UNREPENTANT PATRIOT

The Life and Work of Carl Zuckmayer

Allan Mitchell

Order this book online at www.trafford.com
or email orders@trafford.com

Most Trafford titles are also available at major online book retailers.

All photographs courtesy of the Deutsches Literaturarchiv, Marbach-am-Neckar, Germany.

Print information available on the last page.

ISBN: 978-1-4907-6887-8 (sc)
ISBN: 978-1-4907-6888-5 (hc)
ISBN: 978-1-4907-6892-2 (e)

Library of Congress Control Number: 2016900319

Trafford rev. 02/19/2016

www.trafford.com
North America & international
toll-free: 1 888 232 4444 (USA & Canada)
fax: 812 355 4082

for Annemarie

who has helped me more than she knows,

and who will keep a special place in my affections

"Till all the seas gang dry, my dear,

And the rocks melt with the sun."

CONTENTS

PREFACE

Like many young men of our generation, my initial encounter with Carl Zuckmayer was unconscious but filled with erotic fantasy. It occurred when I saw the film *Der Blaue Engel*, in which the world was first exposed to a generous glimpse of Marlene Dietrich's remarkable gestalt and sultry voice. What I did not know then, and few remember today, was that Zuckmayer had written the screenplay that was adapted from Heinrich Mann's novel, *Professor Unrat*. It was Zuckmayer who thus provided the words that were spoken in a superbly pathetic performance by Emil Jannings and which made la Dietrich an international star. Astonishingly, in his lengthy autobiography (573 pages!) Zuckmayer passes this episode of his career off in a single sentence. The scenario, he claims, was composed merely of "artisanal products, finger exercises, essays."[1] Obviously, he had other things in mind that were far more important to him. The purpose of this brief study is to unravel some of those concerns and to evaluate Zuckmayer's place in the pantheon of twentieth-century playwrights. Above all, it is my intention to introduce him to a reading public that may have only a very faint impression of him or none at all. This is an effort, in other words, to present the essential Zuckmayer.

In reality Zuckmayer had two stories to tell. One was his role as a witness of the tumultuous and tragic events that befell Europe and the United States during his lifetime. Necessarily, he always had one eye on the ambient political and social context of that era, from which he could not have escaped even if he wished to do so. The other tale more specifically examined his part in the evolution of modern theater and cinema in the German-speaking territories of Central Europe. There he became one of Germany's most popular and acclaimed authors, especially known for his cleverly biting satires.

In the biographical Part One of this work it is surely best to proceed in chronological order, even though Zuckmayer himself does not do so in his memoirs. We shall therefore follow his youthful years that climaxed in military service during the First World War, his emergence as a noted writer under the Weimar Republic, the advent of Nazism forcing a flight into exile, and his experience in America before a troubling return to liberated Europe. As it happened, this simple structure was packed with all manner of complexity. Few authors pursued their itinerary in life with equal intensity or succeeded in recounting it with as much telling detail. It is only appropriate that the ensuing Part Two is then devoted to Zuckmayer's writings, his plays and correspondence, since the premise of this book is that both as a witness and as an artist Carl Zuckmayer deserves to be remembered.

Throughout—hence the title of this book—Zuckmayer remained faithful to a vision of his native land that seldom bore much resemblance to the historical reality. The vicissitudes of Germany in the twentieth century acutely scarred him, not alone, and left a deeply engrained ambiguity. To capture a sense of the continuities and disruptions that marked his experience it may be useful to compare this volume with a previous one concerning the life and work of Ernst Jünger.[2] These two authors had remarkably similar backgrounds; yet their participation and perspective in the early twentieth century were entirely different, and it is instructive to inquire how and why that was so. This matter is best deferred to a postscript.

Again, as in the Jünger study, it is my pleasure to thank the staff of the Deutsches Literaturarchiv in Marbach-am-Neckar, especially Heidrun Fink and Thomas Kemme, for their expert assistance in uncovering sources. It was my good fortune as well to benefit from a critical reading of an earlier draft by my lifelong friend, Larry Joseph. I am likewise grateful to Gretchen Ridgeway for her careful proofreading of the entire text. And as always, I am indebted to my two daughters, Catherine and Alexandra, for their love and moral support. Finally, as for my four grandchildren, I can only wish them much happiness and success as they settle into various parts of the world.

A.M.

Boulder, Colorado

PART ONE

THE ACTOR

Chapter One

PEACE AND WAR

"Zuck," as his close friends liked to call him, led a totally
unremarkable youth. And looking back, he did not shrink from
a cliché: "I had a happy childhood."[1] He was born two days after
Christmas in the year 1896 in the Hessian village of Nackenheim
and then moved with his family in 1900 to Mainz, a nearby thriving
commercial town where the Main River flows into the Rhine. His
birth occurred suddenly when his very pregnant mother accidentally
fell down a flight of stairs and thereby left no time for a midwife
to arrive—obviously to no ill effect, since her labor was swiftly and
easily concluded at home. Carl was the second Zuckmayer son, six
years younger than his brother, Eduard.

On both sides his parents and grandparents were solid
German burghers—not wealthy, but rich enough to employ servants.
Zuckmayer's father owned and successfully operated a small factory
that produced wine capsules (to plug bottles after their opening),

3

indispensable items in the heart of the Rhineland. Indeed, the family house stood on the edge of a vineyard, enabling the sons to look out over a large field of grape stocks from their bedroom window. One detail seemingly irrelevant at the time would later be of major significance: the grandparents on Frau Zuckmayer's side bore the name Goldschmidt, suggesting a Jewish background, even though they had converted to Christianity. Apparently, so Carl Zuckmayer recalled, the conversion was not sought for religious reasons but rather symbolized a simple desire to become fully integrated members of the German nation. In Mainz that of course meant a choice of the Roman Catholic faith shared by the vast majority of its citizens. Although he later paid little heed to the Church in matters theological and philosophical, it is fair to say that Carl Zuckmayer remained throughout his life deeply marked in speech and habit by his Rhenish Catholic upbringing. Yet after 1933, needless to insist, his Jewish lineage could no longer be considered inconsequential. Still, it must be emphasized that Mainz had no ghetto or distinctively Jewish quarters, so that Zuckmayer could later testify that he grew up unaware of any notion that racial prejudice would play a part in his progress.

It followed that as a youngster Zuckmayer was admitted to Mainz's finest *Gymnasium* along with other well-clad boys of a certain social standing. There he experienced what he remembered as a kind of class warfare. To reach his high school he needed to pass through a section of town occupied by less privileged "alley kids," who would block his way, sometimes spit at him and his classmates, or even throw stones. Again, this was a social reality that did not deeply mark an adolescent schoolboy and did not begin to reveal its full implications to him until much later.

Otherwise Zuckmayer was the image of normalcy. His patriotism was a gift from his family and taken for granted—they were all Germans and proud of it. Another inherited trait, it appeared, was acquired from his grandfather Zuckmayer, who was handsome, fun-loving, an avid theater buff, and something of a ladies' man. But the bourgeois household was appropriately proper *("ordentlich,"* as the Germans would say), and sex was a taboo subject. Accordingly, this attitude was extended to the schoolroom, where Latin study of classic authors like Homer, Ovid, and Horace was conducted with expurgated versions of the text. As a young pupil Zuckmayer was a daydreamer and displayed a rebellious streak, especially about age fifteen when he discovered Nietzsche and found this new brand of skepticism and humanism at odds with the heretofore unchallenged Catholic dogmas and rituals. In retrospect, most of such fuss does not seem particularly unusual and, if anything, was rather typical for teenagers of that time and place.

Mention should also be made of summer excursions affordable for his parents to Switzerland, South Tyrol, the North Sea coast, and the Netherlands. There is no way to measure how much these trips sparked the imagination or curiosity of a young lad. Certainly they offered some sense of otherness to Zuckmayer, but such travels were largely confined to the Germanic world he already knew. Another limitation was his utter boredom when being dragged through the extraordinary museums of Munich, although he nonetheless gained some initiation to the arts that he would soon begin to appreciate and emulate.

One more factor of incalculable influence was his brother Eduard. Always an outstanding student in school, Eduard appeared destined with intense parental encouragement to pursue a career in law. Instead, he turned to music. Eduard proved to be a talented pianist who was in short order able to outperform his teachers. Albeit less gifted, with fraternal assistance Carl Zuckmayer also obtained a musical education. Before 1914 the city of Mainz, though no metropolis, boasted a symphony hall where he became familiar with Brahms, Mahler, and foremost Wagner, whose *Meistersinger* afforded the greatest frisson of his youth. He was likewise exposed to operettas—naturally among them those by Lehar and Strauss— and to theater productions of authors such as Ibsen, Schnitzler, and Hofmannsthal. His reading list expanded at the same time to include among others: Hauptmann, Wedekind, Rilke, and Kafka. Notable as well was a visit in Frankfurt to see one of the earliest exhibitions by painters rapidly gaining in reputation, such as Marc, Macke, Kandinsky, and Chagall.

It is not too much, then, to observe that the late Kaiserreich was undergoing a kind of cultural renaissance before the First World War and thus enjoyed its own Belle Époque. This was as well the age of those intrepid hikers and campers, the *Wandervogel*, whom young Zuckmayer joined; and of the first automobiles, airplanes, and zeppelins that stirred countless young imaginations, decidedly including that of Carl Zuckmayer: "we were underway, we could no longer turn back."[2]

All of this, the world of yesterday, came to an abrupt conclusion in August 1914. As Zuckmayer was much later to put it so poignantly in his memoirs: "The dream and [my] youth came to an end. Fate had spoken . . ."[3] Like thousands of other young men of his age, he promptly volunteered for military service, even though his schooling was as yet unfinished. To clear the path he was awarded an "emergency diploma" *(Notabitur)* after passing a perfunctory test at his *Gymnasium.* After all, what misguided teacher would flunk a youngster who was setting off into a battle from which he might never return? And many did not.

Before departing Zuckmayer had two matters of unfinished business to tend. The first was Annemarie Ganz, his high school sweetheart. A Teutonic blonde, blue-eyed, smart, and cute, she was an ideal and eminently desirable first mate—albeit not, as it turned out, a suitable partner for life. The two would be married right after the

7

war, an ill-fated arrangement that lasted scarcely a year. Meanwhile, Zuckmayer was trying his hand as a fledgling author. He composed a cycle of poetry, and in a moment of bravado—only days before Austria declared war on Serbia—sent it off to the prestigious *Frankfurter Zeitung.* To his amazement, the newspaper agreed to publish his work; but in the midst of military mobilization, when everything was in flux, it was lost in the confusion. Forty years later he inadvertently rediscovered his hand-written manuscript.

Zuckmayer's feelings about the outbreak of the European conflict are difficult to define. The general spirit in Mainz at that moment was not so much military as revolutionary, that is, drenched with the sense of a struggle for Germany's freedom from surrounding foes. Decades before, Otto von Bismarck had warned of the dangers of encirclement by enemies, and now that circumstance was at hand. This sentiment was not incompatible with another: a wish for the unity of the German people. The dramatic pronouncement of Kaiser Wilhelm II in early August 1914 that he no longer knew parties, only Germans, was taken at face value; and the German Social Democratic Party reciprocated by voting for war credits. Hence Zuckmayer hoped Germany would not only be free but also become more democratic in effect under a constitutional monarchy. To say the least, these thoughts were imprecise, and they were basically unpolitical.

Behind these dominating emotions there was a third and perhaps less laudable ambition: at last to defeat the French once and for all. Trains heading to the western front bore the banners: "Free Excursion to Paris," a destination they would not quite reach. In the background, Russia remained the great unknown.

Zuckmayer and his generation, in short, were swept up in a miasma of idealism much like the passion of a young lover who knows not yet what love means, and who ignores that heartbreak and sadness are an inseparable part of it. Neither was there any room here for a fear of death. Come what might, along with his fellow recruits, Carl Zuckmayer was prepared to sacrifice everything for the *Vaterland*, unfathomable future be damned.

So Carl Zuckmayer donned a field gray uniform. German spirits were running high as the stunning reports came rolling in: Belfort, Reims, Lille, and Antwerp fell to the invading forces, just as General von Schlieffen had planned, and German troops were advancing rapidly toward the Marne. The eastern front was harder to evaluate, but also there an initial string of tactical victories seemed to bode well. The one disturbing note of the first weeks was the entry of Great Britain as an ally of France. Zuckmayer was among those to believe the tale that Germany had not actually provoked the British by the invasion of Belgium. Rather, the wily Belgians had purposely opened the way for French attacks on their left flank, thereby rendering a German preemptive strike necessary. And as the

Chancellor Bethmann-Hollweg cogently observed: "Necessity knows no law."

Zuckmayer was usually not one to speak of war or to recount his adventures in it, which he considered incomprehensible to those without direct experience of military combat. Yet the record is not entirely blank, since one chapter of his memoirs testifies to the noise, the smells, the confusion and fatigue, the cold or heat that daily suffused the western front for the next four years. At the outset he wanted to join the cavalry, cleaning stalls, grooming, feeding, and riding horses. Instead, he was soon assigned to a field artillery unit headquartered in Darmstadt. Finally, under a copious hail of flowers, cigarettes, and chocolates tossed out of windows by the local girls, his regiment was shipped off to France.

Zuckmayer learned to survive. He also found that his erstwhile comrades were not always well-disposed toward him—as when, after he had accidentally tipped over a pot of coffee, a huge fellow private smacked him right in the face. He saw death at first hand when a soldier standing next to him was struck by a bullet to the head, "his face transformed into a bloody mess."[4] He was given a first promotion and moved to a commando in the forward trenches, where he laid telephone lines and fired cannons. More than once he faced charging hostile troops across open terrain. He slept outside, yes, amid the poppies in Flanders fields. He was scarcely eighteen when this action started, twenty-one when it ended.

The war changed Zuckmayer in significant ways. He met all manner of young men from all regions and social strata with different idioms and dialects. He lost his hatred of enemies on the other side, dressed in steel gray or khaki: "the foe, for all of us, was the war."[5] Above all, he felt alone even with others, even in combat; and he was certain that, if he were killed, it was sure to be a lonely death. That loneliness followed him on furlough. He was granted leave five times (three of which were cut short by orders to return to the front) during those four years. Yet, even among family and friends, he was unable to communicate his experience or shake a sense of alienation.

The war went on. He was promoted up through the ranks and became Lieutenant Zuckmayer. This meant better living conditions and more leisure time. He used his new status to read voraciously and to visit museums in Belgium and northern France. Besides art history, he studied economics (Adam Smith, Ricardo, Louis Blanc, Feuerbach, Proudhon, Marx, Max Weber), French literature (Rimbaud, Verlaine, Montaigne, Flaubert), classic dramas and novels (Strindberg, Swift, Dickens, Tolstoi, Dostoevsky), theology and philosophy (Plato, Augustine, Aquinas, Descartes, Hegel, Schopenhauer), the Reformation (Hutten, Erasmus, Luther), and so on. He even found time for some occasional writing. On a whim he sent two poems to a Berlin left-wing pacifist journal, *Aktion*, and was surprised when, without notification, his pieces were published—his first appearance in print. Again, a coherent description of his evolving mentality is difficult to formulate. Although still in uniform, he had become profoundly anti-war. He wanted some sort of spiritual revolution in Germany without having any notion of what form a political upheaval, if ever it came, could take. He heard reports of insurrectionary events in Russia, but he remained only vaguely aware of conditions there. In sum, it appears that Zuckmayer approached the postwar world as unknowingly as he had left the prewar.

As the war entered a critical phase, half of the men in Zuckmayer's unit were dead or seriously wounded. Now there were new long distance artillery weapons. As before, his duties included observation of the effects of bombardment, with the innovation that this activity required perilous flight in balloons and aircraft. But this was soon made useless by the growing superiority of the allies and Americans. One positive note was his meeting with an air force officer, Ernst Udet. The two were to become thick friends for the next twenty years, a matter to which we must return.

After the German retreat from the Somme, tanks now ruled the battlefields, and the proverbial handwriting was scrawled on the walls of eastern France. As he later wrote, "the war was lost, and we knew it."[6] The Ludendorff offensive in the spring of 1918 was Germany's last chance. Once more in Flanders that May, Zuckmayer wrote a letter: "Briefly in Lille. Schnaps. Whores. Drinking. Armentières: blood, death, blood . . .and the worst: alone."[7] One notable personal event was a brief encounter with Kaiser Wilhelm II at a ceremony honoring a soldier awarded the Iron Cross. Standing only a few steps away from the leader he had so enthusiastically supported in 1914, Zuckmayer was shocked by the appearance of the Kaiser's grim ashen face, "a tragic mask" that he would never forget.[8]

In July 1918 the observation post where Zuckmayer was on duty received the direct hit of an artillery shell, and he was left for dead. Somehow he managed to survive with a shrapnel wound above his left eye and a throbbing concussion. After a week in a field infirmary, he was sent home, where he promptly collapsed. Thereupon he was transferred to a hospital ward in a Franciscan monastery near Mainz. Although not fully recovered, he was dispatched once more to a new unit at the front beyond Strasbourg in the Vosges Mountains. There he was immediately drawn into a radical soldiers' council (*Soldatenrat*), but it is noteworthy that they did not sing "*Die Internationale*" but instead "*In der Heimat, in der Heimat.*" With a red armband tied to his uniform, he and his remaining troops finally withdrew across the bridge between Strasbourg and Kehl, back into Germany. At last the war was over. "Starving, beaten, but with our weapons, we marched home."[9]

Chapter Two

THE WEIMAR YEARS

Carl Zuckmayer had two stories to tell about postwar
Germany. One recorded his perception of the constantly changing
circumstances of the troubled and unstable Weimar Republic. Another
concerned the world of German theater and his own progress in it
as a playwright. The two were of course tightly intertwined, and in
constructing his much later memoirs, Zuckmayer mixed them into his
ongoing narrative, passing from one to the other and back again as he
deemed appropriate. In the interest of clarity, however, it would be well
to separate these twin themes and to treat them successively.

Germany experienced no revolution in 1918, Zuckmayer
believed, but suffered a military collapse followed by a few years of
public disorientation that finally closed with a currency reform and the
introduction of the so-called *Rentenmark* in 1923. This period began in
late October 1918 with a mutiny in the port city of Kiel by sailors who
refused to ship out into what was essentially a suicide mission against

an overwhelming British sea power. Then on November 7 came an uprising in Munich that upset the Wittelsbach dynasty there, a prelude to rioting in Berlin two days later that forced the Kaiser to flee to the Netherlands, signaling an end to the German Empire. Yet there was no victory of a revolutionary party. Instead, the Social Democrats came to the fore, which under the chaotic conditions of that moment meant that the new regime would pledge to support parliamentary democracy. The model of Lenin's Soviet Russia proved to be a mirage in Germany. Communism and radical socialistic tendencies thus had no chance to lead a defeated and disillusioned German nation that longed for nothing more than peace and quiet after four years of warfare. At a dramatic December meeting in Berlin the revolutionary councils of workers and soldiers in effect voted themselves out of existence. After the Spartacist leaders Karl Liebknecht and Rosa Luxemburg were assassinated, the modest and moderate SPD leader Friedrich Ebert— who had lost two sons for his fatherland in the war—was elected as the first president of the Weimar Republic. This scenario is now altogether familiar to historians of modern Germany and is nowhere seriously contested. Zuckmayer did not challenge it.

He had marched back to Mainz where, without much ado, Grossherzog Ernst Ludwig of Hesse was replaced by a socialist administration that lasted through the ensuing decade and a half of republican hegemony. The initial four or five years were anything

15

but comfortable, marked as they were by shortages of food, coal, and electricity; economic distress and labor strikes; and uncertainties at every hand. Nonetheless, Zuckmayer greeted the advent of a new era positively and hopefully. The war was gone, and with it the killing and maiming and the constantly oppressive dread of sudden death.

After helping his mother to rescue his severely wounded brother Eduard in Bremen—which could be reached only by a nightmarish succession of short train rides—Zuckmayer was at last able to shed his uniform for good and to enroll as a student at the University of Frankfurt-am-Main, a short distance from Mainz. There, at the behest of his father, he intended to concentrate on Roman law and classical economics for which, however, he acquired no appetite and little interest. He did become politically active by joining a "Revolutionary Student Council" at the university and by accepting an invitation to become a staff member of the leftist journal *Das Tribunal*. This debut came to nothing after he was roughly ejected from a public meeting in which he vainly attempted to defend an unpopular strike of local workers. Thereupon he quit the university and moved on to Heidelberg.

At the University of Heidelberg Zuckmayer began more humbly, joining with his two friends Carlo Mierendorff and Theo Heubach in a veterans' organization. What its members shared in common, besides their war experience, was an interest in politics, art, philosophy, and sports. They were not socialist in name but in orientation. They were also mostly poor, a recurrent problem for Zuckmayer until after the Second World War. His father's business declined after 1918 when, half blind, he was forced into retirement. More often than not, as a student, Zuckmayer consequently lived on an uninspiring diet of which the highlights were canned milk, corned beef, and cheap wine. In Heidelberg he lived in a little attic room. Still, he was able to renew his romance with his girlfriend, Annemarie Ganz, with whom he enjoyed frequent excursions into the green and lush Rhine-Main region to visit the surrounding villages, cloisters, churches, museums, and towns (Worms, Mannheim, as far as Karlsruhe), plus strolls along Heidelberg's famous *Philosophen-Weg.* His friends and acquaintances were much too numerous and various to mention here at any length, but they included such future luminaries as Paul Hindemith, Oskar Kokoschka, the sociologist (brother of Max) Alfred Weber, and...Joseph Goebbels. As for his studies, Zuckmayer admittedly lacked the patience for systematic learning, and he had no precise ambition except to soak up German culture. Faute de mieux, then, he turned to biology and zoology, to little effect.

For reasons of his professional life (of which more later), in 1922 Zuckmayer prepared to move away from the Rhineland to Berlin and Munich, where he would have a first-hand view of the halting evolution of the Weimar Republic, which frankly he found "depressing and miserable."[1] His worst fears were confirmed in that June by the assassination in Berlin of Walther Rathenau, Germany's

17

foreign minister and, not coincidentally, most prominent Jew. This occurred just before Zuckmayer's departure from Heidelberg, where the university was briefly closed while flags were flown at half mast. A silent procession of townspeople marched in Rathenau's honor on the day of his burial. But that evening a counter-demonstration of university fraternity brothers chanted in unison:

"Verreckt ist Walther Rathenau

Die gottverdammte Judensau,"

which can be translated without the rhyme:

"Eradicated is Walther Rathenau

The goddamned Jewish pig."

Zuckmayer could only comment: "We heard the voice of the murderers."[2]

His private life was also in turmoil. His amorous relationship with Annemarie Ganz, so suddenly and cruelly interrupted by the war, resumed thereafter and was sealed by marriage in January 1920 in an attempt to recapture the past. Yet it did not work out. "It could not succeed," Zuckmayer rationalized, "because there is no way back."[3] There was another crucial factor, a second Annemarie, a young actress he met shortly after arriving in Berlin and with whom he promptly began a passionate affair. Zuckmayer's divorce from his first wife thereby became unavoidable. With Annemarie Seidel, called "Mirl," it was love at first sight. There were immediate thoughts of marriage, encouraged by a trip to Munich to visit her family. But back in Berlin

Mirl developed a hacking cough, resulting, as they learned, from a serious lung infection. She needed rest and fresh air, preferably in a Swiss sanatorium, something Zuckmayer could not possibly offer her. A mutual friend, as it happened a Dutch millionaire, could and did. She parted with him to Davos; and, as Zuckmayer sadly but definitively concluded, "that was the end."[4]

After a brief and inglorious episode in Kiel, Zuckmayer returned to Munich in 1923. There he gained a close and sobering glimpse of the shocking events that were engulfing Central Europe. The German inflation was reaching its peak, paramilitary vigilante *Freikorps* units were roaming the streets, the French army occupied the Ruhr, while reports of a separatist movement in the Rhineland became ominous. And there in Munich was Adolf Hitler with his brown shirts. Zuckmayer was not alone to be both fascinated and repulsed by Hitler's thumping rampages at rowdy Munich beer hall gatherings, which he several times attended. He considered the Nazi Führer to be "a screaming Dervish," whose speeches evinced "barbaric-primitive effectiveness."[5]

Without question, no surprise, anti-Semitism was clearly the most persistent note in every performance, since in Hitler's version of recent history "the Jew" was primarily to blame for Germany's military defeat and the humiliation of Versailles. The climax came on November 9 when Nazi storm troopers, Bavarian police officers, and curious onlookers thronged through the boulevards of Munich.

Zuckmayer was in the midst of the crowd, a direct witness to the showdown that took place at the Odeonsplatz, which ended in stark confusion with competing orators, skirmishes, and gunfire. After Hitler was wounded and arrested, with his minions scattered, he was sent off to detention at the nearby fortress of Landsberg, where he was to dictate the manuscript of *Mein Kampf*, to which no one at the time— Zuckmayer included—paid much attention. As far as one could tell, Nazism was finished.

Evidently, then, by the end of 1923 the Weimar Republic had passed through the most extreme moment of tension. The *Rentenmark* was introduced, ending the worst of inflation and apparently stabilizing the German economy. A genuine republican, Gustav Stresemann, took charge of the government and secured the French withdrawal from the Ruhr. The Republic could at last begin over again in relative peace and prosperity. And Carl Zuckmayer could make his way back to Berlin to begin his career in earnest. It can by no means be said that Zuckmayer's entry into the world of theater there was a rousing success. To the contrary, in the beginning he was forced to endure one stinging disappointment after another. Inauspicious is the word. While nominally enrolled as a student at the university in Frankfurt, his main interest was undoubtedly elsewhere, namely in the city's thriving theater scene, second perhaps only to that of Berlin. As a neophyte he observed it at the outset from a distant balcony seat, which he did night after night. Meanwhile his days were often passed writing sketches for an imaginary grandiose spectacle, stretching from ancient Greece to Soviet Russia, or as he said, from Prometheus to Lenin. Although this exceedingly ambitious project was never realized, it did bring him into contact with some of Frankfurt's literary lions, who offered occasional words of encouragement. They also had suggestions, one of which was to focus on a play featuring the Roman slave Spartacus in a modern factory setting as the leader of the proletariat. This, too, remained a pipe dream, since it did not take Zuckmayer long to realize that his talents were ill- suited to promoting a political theater that dwelled on revolutionary proclamations. He did manage to finish one drama in Heidelberg, entitled *Kreuzweg*, which led to his decision "with my last money" to try his luck back in Berlin.[6]

Famously, it was the Protestant, Henry of Navarre, who said "Paris is worth a mass" when he converted to Catholicism in order to become the French King Henri IV. For Carl Zuckmayer Berlin was worth more than a mass, as he recalled years later. A city of extraordinary vitality, swarming with gifted young aspirants, it was also home to countless scoundrels and pretenders whose machinations made it difficult to sort out those persons of real substance in a constant process of winnowing. The attempt to begin a career there would be risky, but he would take his chances, convinced as he was that "the world belonged to whoever had Berlin."[7]

21

Zuckmayer soon learned whereof he spoke. By a stroke of seeming good luck, his maiden dramatic effort *Kreuzweg* was not only accepted for publication but also to be performed at the famous Deutsches Theater on the Gendarmenmarkt, the very center of German cultural life. He was all of twenty-four years old when he arrived at Berlin's Anhalter Bahnhof, excited and filled with high expectations. Six weeks went by before the premier, which proved to be a catastrophe. His play was ridiculed and condemned by critics. "This incurable poet," wrote the lead tenor of the Berlin press, Alfred Kerr, "will never produce a speakable sentence on the stage." The production closed after three performances, the third of which played before a nearly empty house. Zuckmayer had to concede that "it was a complete defeat."[8]

Yet he was undeterred, determined to carry on, though he was now "without money, without position, without fame."[9] No longer concerned to pursue university studies, he would remain in Berlin. His life would be the theater, possibly also the cinema. The only other feasible possibility, in the days before radio and television, was the political cabaret, for which the German capital was justly famed. But that was not for him. Rather, he continued to write scenes for never produced plays, poetic fragments, and an occasional essay.

His brief stay in Munich with Annemarie Seidel did not appreciably alter matters. He lived there in Schwabing, absorbing what he could of the Bavarian capital's art, theater, and literary activity, and then moved back to Berlin. Unable to finish any project, he took odd jobs, for example once playing a soldier in a silent film. One advantage was an opportunity to learn Berlin dialect, which he would later put to good use. That future was not obviously in sight. He bided his time by becoming a *"Schlepper,"* that is, one who picks up single gentlemen on the streets in the evening and coaxes them into nearby nightclubs. It went with the territory that he became marginally involved in the drug trade and narrowly escaped arrest in the Tauentzienstrasse near the Wittenbergplatz.[10]

It was about this time that some good fortune finally appeared to beckon Carl Zuckmayer. During a short visit to see his parents in Mainz he met an acquaintance who had there been director of the municipal theater and who had recently accepted the call to a similar post in Kiel. He needed an assistant and offered the position to Zuckmayer. Another catastrophe ensued. Tired of the reigning dramas of German Expressionism, he attempted to promote a sort of trendy experimental theater in Kiel. It was a move that pleased neither the public nor many of the resident actors. Receipts declined and protests grew. The denouement came when Zuckmayer adapted and directed a modem version of *Der Eunuch* by the second-century Roman dramatist Terrence. The language was vulgar and the staging risqué, including nudity. After the premier the audience left the theater in ominous silence. The municipal council of Kiel was convened, and it voted to have the production removed from the playbill. Zuckmayer and his friend from Mainz were then dismissed.[11]

Zuckmayer's second and longer residence in Munich in 1923 was no more brilliant. He did not succeed in mounting a production of *Der Eunuch* as he had hoped. Penurious as before, he did manage to gain employment at a minimal salary at a theater in the Maximilianstrasse. There he met Klaus and Erika Mann, plus a host of young actors and playwrights, most notable among them Bertolt Brecht. Both born entertainers, they immediately struck up an intimate relationship that began in a pub with passing a guitar back and forth to sing ribald songs. They often walked together along the Isar River or in the English Garden, and they sat up in the evenings talking and drinking. But there were limits. Zuckmayer identified Brecht, age twenty-five, as a true genius, but he simultaneously recognized his friend's will to dominate others. It was not safe to become too close. At that juncture Brecht was less interested in German politics, and he was not as radical—except in his writing. He even drove carefully in Munich's downtown traffic. Thus "he generally lived quietly and without excess," something Zuckmayer could not well say of himself.[12]

Then came a break. Zuckmayer and Brecht were invited together to serve as assistants in Max Reinhardt's team at the Deutsches Theater. For Zuckmayer it meant a return to Berlin's Gendarmenmarkt, a second chance. This time, although he was still composing failed dramas, he would stay. He and Brecht had adjoining offices. When promenading Unter den Linden they found that the city had been spruced up after the crises of 1923 were resolved. The postwar shabbiness was disappearing as facades were repainted and show windows became more opulently decorated. Zuckmayer also participated in a youth theater and there experienced his second premier, another failure. This play was called *Pankraz erwacht,* a bubble that his nemesis Alfred Kerr was quick to burst, calling it eminently forgettable.[13] Yet again Zuckmayer was still undismayed. Although he and Brecht were fired, they continued to believe that they each had a future in the theater. And we know that their belief was altogether justified.

Still penniless and without steady income, Zuckmayer was taken in by a cousin of his mother, a rich Berlin banker with a waterfront estate on the Wannsee just west of the city. There he resided in a large attic room where he was able, undisturbed, to write his first successful play, *Der fröhliche Weinberg (The Merry Vineyard).*[14] It was the autumn of 1925, at the same time when he also met an Austrian woman he would soon marry, Alice Frank née Herdan. Zuckmayer's play, which could be described as a rowdy farce, was written in his native Mainz-Frankfurt dialect and deliberately caricatured various German types, exposing their foibles and pomposities. Apparently considered too rustic for the sophisticated Berlin stage, it was initially rejected by several theaters there. Yet it was published and, to Zuckmayer's astonishment, was awarded the

Kleist Prize, then the most prestigious honor possible for a young playwright (Brecht had won it two years earlier). With his prize money Zuckmayer immediately purchased new clothes and a lavish dinner. In the meantime his play went into production at the elegant Theater am Schiffbauerdamm and had its premier shortly before Christmas 1925. "Happiness. Success," he exclaimed. In the press critics were positive, even Alfred Kerr, who was seated at the premier next to Zuckmayer's mother. *Der fröhliche Weinberg* played at the same theater for the next two and a half years.[15]

It was also a huge triumph in Frankfurt, where the local dialect was much appreciated, not to mention the randy behavior and political satire of the piece. In succeeding years it was often performed in smaller towns in all of Germany, though not without some pointed objections. The depiction of a pretentious university student drew a negative response from conservative fraternities. Some viewers were also offended by Zuckmayer's use of family names that were common in the Mainz region, as if he were singling out certain individuals. And the intentional satire of ultra-nationalism was predictably condemned by the Nazi Party. All of which provided common ground with Thomas Mann, whom Zuckmayer first met at this juncture, since similar problems had arisen regarding Mann's fictitious Buddenbrook family in his home town of Lübeck.

In 1926, now married and with some cash on hand, Zuckmayer learned of an abandoned mill in Austria near Salzburg, the landscape of Alice Zuckmayer's origin. This "Wiesmühl" in Henndorf had not been occupied for two decades and had neither electricity nor running water, hence no kitchen or bath. But they determined to buy it, and in coming years they spent much of every year there with Michaela, Alice's child from her first marriage, and their own daughter, whimsically named Maria Winnetou. They meanwhile maintained an apartment in Berlin, located beside the Schöneberger Stadtpark, enabling Zuckmayer to extend his career in German theater.

Frequently commuting between Berlin and Henndorf (where he did most of his writing), Zuckmayer enhanced his reputation with what may be described as a string of moderately successful dramas in the late 1920s. His *Schinderhannes* premiered in the Lessing Theater in 1927 and quickly became a staple of provincial houses thereafter. In 1928 *Katharina Knie* appeared, written like *Der fröhliche Weinberg* in Rhenish dialect, which earned him another accolade with the Georg Büchner Prize.[16] But the crowning achievement, the one for which he is best remembered, was *Der Hauptmann von Köpenick*. This delightful comedy recounted an episode that had occurred two decades before when a civilian donned the uniform of a Prussian officer and began barking orders to one and all. Written down within two months in Henndorf, the finished manuscript was presented by Zuckmayer to the famous director Max Reinhardt in Berlin. The premier was staged at the Deutsches Theater in March 1931. Unquestionably it was Zuckmayer's greatest hit, which the author himself considered "deeper and more enduring" than *Der fröhliche Weinberg.* In later years, after the Second World War, it would be filmed no fewer than four times. Decidedly, Carl Zuckmayer had arrived.[17]

The foregoing two narratives—Carl Zuckmayer's observation of the erratic course of German politics and the account of his emergence as a mainstay of German theater—came abruptly into collision in the early 1930s. By then the Nazis were already on the march again, and Zuckmayer soon found that he was a marked man. Although he had known Joseph Goebbels only very slightly as a student, Zuckmayer's early writings had not escaped the future propaganda chief's notice. It was well-known that some of his first journalistic essays were conspicuously leftist. For right-wing radicals, as noted, *Der fröhliche Weinberg,* with its ridicule of their pretensions, had been nothing more than a succès de scandale, to which was added Zuckmayer's highly favorable review of Erich Maria Remarque's anti-war novel *Im Westen nichts Neues (All Quiet on the Western Front)* in 1928. Because of a prison scene, even Zuckmayer's hilarious *Der Hauptmann von Köpenick* was viciously attacked by the Berlin journal *Der Angriff,* edited by Goebbels, who suggested none too subtly that Zuckmayer himself might before long become personally acquainted with the interior of a Prussian jailhouse. But he made no attempt to hide his political proclivities. He briefly joined the leftist Iron Front, the only political organization since his student days to which he ever belonged, thereby identifying himself with the opposition to Nazism. And he spoke in the Prussian parliament against censorship of the film version of Remarque's writings.

The rise of Adolf Hitler—one might almost call it his political resurrection after the fiasco of 1923 in Munich—was perplexing to Zuckmayer. Both had fought and suffered for their country. Zuckmayer's patriotism was unflagging and never in question. Yet in his own fashion Hitler was also a patriot, albeit one who still felt deeply resentful of Versailles and who espoused a radical anti-Semitic racism that was foreign to Zuckmayer. With his career blossoming, Zuckmayer was proud to be a German and wanted to remain in Germany. Moreover, he also did not believe the worst could happen: "I consider a war to be impossible at least for fifty years, as well as a real upheaval in Germany," he wrote in 1931. But Hitler's elevation to the chancellorship in January 1933 and the impending dictatorial rule of the Nazi Party would soon prove him wrong.[18]

Chapter Three

THE NAZI YEARS

One must be clear about Carl Zuckmayer's flight from Germany. His immediate problem was not a Jewish heritage through his mother but rather his anti-fascist literary activity despised by the Nazi Party. After all, he was married to a Gentile; and we know for example from the brilliant memoirs of Victor Klemperer how special provisions for mixed Christian/Jewish marriages were quite possible, temporarily at least, after 1933. Zuckmayer's own parents managed to live in Germany, modestly but unharmed, for the entire period up to 1945. Thus it is fair to conclude, as it were, that Zuckmayer's first threat was not so much from Heinrich Himmler as Joseph Goebbels.

However that may have been, Zuckmayer had to take seriously the admonition that he was "in the greatest danger" if he did not leave Germany.[1] He had no desire to emigrate, but it seemed by far the most prudent course of action. But where should he go? The answer was obvious: to the old mill in Henndorf. The Zuckmayers had purchased the Wiesmühl in 1926 and often resided there for long stretches since then. It had already become home for them and was to remain so for a while after Hitler's *Machtergreifung* in January 1933. In addition, they acquired an apartment in Vienna in 1935 as a surrogate for their lost dwelling in Berlin, confiscated by the Nazis. Meanwhile *Der fröhliche Weinberg, Der Hauptmann von Köpenick*, and Zuckmayer's other plays were banned throughout Germany. Only three weeks before the Nazi takeover Zuckmayer had received Austrian citizenship. But fortunately he never received his new passport, which was discovered after 1945 in a Salzburg police station with an attached memo from the Gestapo: the owner should be arrested at once.

In some respects Henndorf was less than ideal—hence the apartment in Vienna. The only way to reach Salzburg was to cross a lake by boat and then to catch a pokey local train. Zuckmayer nonetheless managed to maintain and indeed to enhance his contacts in the theater. The list of his personal encounters with eminent persons was accordingly long. Because he was engaged in writing the screen play for *Der Blaue Engel* at that time, he met the author Heinrich Mann and the lead actor Emil Jannings, and also another famous theater star of the day, Werner Krauss. He became a close friend of Stefan Zweig, who visited Henndorf and drew Zuckmayer into his Austrian circle, besides offering him the gift of a prized tile stove *(Kakelofen)* for the millhouse as well as two handsome dogs, Flick and Flock. In the meantime, through Zweig, he befriended Joseph

Roth, Bruno Walter, and Arturo Toscanini. To those were appended in Salzburg such illustrious personalities as Gerhart Hauptmann, Thomas Mann, Franz Werfel, and Bruno Frank. Without question, this cluster of international all-stars was gratifying, yet Zuckmayer could not suppress a growing sense that it could not last. It was, as he wrote, like living in Versailles before the Bastille.[2]

In early 1938 Austrian chancellor Kurt von Schuschnigg met with Hitler at the Obersalzberg. In retrospect, the reality was essentially the former's capitulation. To put a good face on it, however, Schuschnigg called for a referendum to be held on March 13. When it seemed likely that the outcome might favor an independent Austria, rejected by the Germans, Hitler decided to make a move. On March 11 German troops crossed the border. The Anschluss of Austria within the Third Reich thereby became inevitable.

How did Zuckmayer react? He was now an Austrian citizen and at first appeared unconcerned. On the morning of March 11 he was in Vienna attending a rehearsal of his new drama, *Bellman* (which, as it turned out, did not have its premier until November 1938 in Zürich). That evening Kurt von Schuschnigg made a final radio broadcast of farewell, after which he was promptly arrested.[3] Conditions were chaotic, reminding Zuckmayer of the world according to Hieronymus Bosch. Some of his friends departed that night. "I did not want to." He preferred to return to Henndorf, but his wife knew that was too dangerous and persuaded him to flee instead. In truth, yet again, he had no choice. Unknown to him or his wife, the mill in Henndorf was already occupied by the Nazis.[4]

Zuckmayer's escape had all the trappings of a spy thriller. Hundreds of German aircraft had landed at the Vienna airport. Arrests began: Jews, aristocrats, intellectuals, overt supporters of Austrian independence. Dwellings were searched, more arrests were made, unfortunates were mistreated. The day after Zuckmayer left Vienna his apartment there was cleaned out, including a personal library of several thousand volumes, which he never saw again. He was traveling on a train from Vienna to Zürich with a connection to London, where he had a contract for film work with Alexander Korda, a perfect alibi. He used his German passport instead of the Austrian one, which was lost and which might have in any case aroused suspicions. His train edged along the Wallersee right by Henndorf—he imagined he heard his dogs barking —and passed by a German convoy heading in the opposite direction to Vienna.[5] There was a brief delay in Salzburg, where the train station was filled with German troops. He reached Innsbruck, three hours from the Swiss border, and was there interrogated by an Austrian officer wearing a swastika armband and backed by two brown shirts. After a thorough search of his suitcases, he was let go in time to catch a night train to the border. He underwent another control, this time by a German official. His bags were emptied out and inspected again. Questioned by an SS officer, who recognized his name from the passport and asked him to state the reason why he was not a Nazi Party member, he explained: because his plays were banned in Germany. Astonishingly, for that frankness he was praised by the officer and released. Once more he boarded a coach. "I sat in a train, and it was not going in the direction of Dachau." Months later, commenting in a letter on his narrow escape, he added simply: "I want to survive."[6]

Carl Zuckmayer's thoughts on leaving his homeland were gloomy. Looking back, he found the most important thing in his life were his friends, especially Germans. When one of them died, whatever the circumstances, it was "as if it were a part of me" — the title of his memoirs. In this way he expressed much the same sentiment as had the poet John Donne: "Therefore never send to know for whom the bell tolls; it tolls for thee." Zuckmayer was an eminently convivial man. He had chosen emigration, but it was an act that brought him an overwhelming sadness as he was separated from those he loved. And Switzerland did not prove to be particularly welcoming. Understandably, the Swiss were concerned about being inundated by an immense wave of German refugees who might request expensive social assistance from their tiny neighboring land. Moreover, in the capital city of Bern, where Zuckmayer went to put his papers in order, he detected "outbreaks of anti-Semitism and sympathy for the Nazis."[7] Of course, there were individual exceptions. But he reckoned it would be impossible to remain for long, and he was haunted by dreams of

America. Still, being a European, he preferred somehow to stay in Europe. "What should we do in a land where they squirt ketchup onto beef?"[8] He knew scarcely a word of English. And the situation seemed not yet completely hopeless to one, like himself, who wanted to believe that the Maginot Line would render France invulnerable. This was months before the Munich Agreement, after which such illusions began to crumble.

"We were still not uprooted."[9] In May 1938 Zuckmayer and his wife took up residence in the village of Chardonne, overlooking Lake Geneva, boarding in a small hotel ("Belle-Vue") where Victor Hugo had briefly sought exile during the reign of Napoleon III. From there Zuckmayer was able to travel, several times visiting London and Paris. He spent much of that autumn in Zürich preparing for the premier of his play *Bellman* (received by the Swiss public with some indifference). In London he encountered Lord Vansittart, anti-German and impolite, and met other more measured political figures like Duff Cooper and Harold Nicholson. One British MP astonished him by calling Hitler "quite a good chap," who was valiantly defending western Europe against Soviet communism.

It was in Paris where Zuckmayer was confronted with the European reality. Not that he was personally suffering—as when, for instance, he dined at Maxim's with Friedrich Sieburg, or when he stood before Notre Dame to hear the pronouncement of *"Habemus Papam"* marking Cardinal Pacelli's elevation as Pope Pius XII. Nevertheless, he could not overlook the swastikas painted inside Parisian pissoirs or the walls on which were scrawled "Death to the Jews." Nor could he ignore the threatening implications of the Munich Agreement in that autumn. Since then, he wrote, "we awake with a feeling of revulsion, disgust, senselessness. [Neville] Chamberlain has completely sold out not only the Czechs but Europe."[11] Above all, he was dismayed by the false optimism of the French, firm in their conviction that they possessed the greatest army in the world. Needing an extension of his visa, Zuckmayer visited the office of Jean Giraudoux at the Quai d'Orsay, where he was a ranking staff member of the French diplomatic corps. Giraudoux expressed his belief, because of Munich, that war would not erupt on the continent. Increasingly skeptical, Zuckmayer left the office with, for the first time, a firm determination "to leave Europe as soon as possible."[12] His earlier optimism had evaporated as he assessed the narrowing options left to Germany and Europe. "In the long run there is only one alternative: either war—or unrestrained growth of power and domination by the dictators."[13]

"My sole objective was now to escape before it was too late. There was no time to waste."[14] In need of a visitor's visa to the United States, Zuckmayer traveled to Geneva. From there he and his family headed toward Rotterdam. On the way they stopped in Paris. On their last evening there, so Zuckmayer remembered, he and his wife dined at a fancy restaurant, Vert Galant, on the Île St. Louis. At midnight they ended the evening quite drunk on a bridge (probably the Pont des Arts), staring off into the city lights and listening to the peal of bells from Notre Dame, not knowing whether to laugh or cry. Zuckmayer looked down onto the flowing current of the Seine and imagined that he was standing above the Rhine.[15]

In Rotterdam the Zuckmayer clan boarded the Dutch steamship Zaandam (which would be used in the war as a troop transport and later sunk by the Japanese). Alice's daughter Michaela was left in England at a girls' boarding school. Thus they were four: Carl, Alice, daughter Winnetou (age 11), and Alice's old dog Mucki (age 16, toothless and blind). They had left their silver, jewelry, and furs behind; but the dog (who had two more years to live in exile) had to go with them. Carl Zuckmayer's two dogs were taken in by friends in Henndorf.

With only the most rudimentary grasp of the English language, Zuckmayer needed instruction; and he received it on shipboard by taking lessons from an American actress, Peggy Wood, who would later translate his play *Bellman*. During the voyage Zuckmayer received a cable from the sophisticated and widely respected American journalist, Dorothy Thompson, whom he had first met at a Berlin restaurant in 1925 before he became a successful playwright. She had nonetheless taken an interest in him, and they exchanged visits in the years that followed. On occasion Zuckmayer spent evenings chatting with Thompson in her Berlin apartment. She had arrived in Germany as a young woman and by then spoke fluent if somewhat broken German. Lively and charming, she was (except for her bothersome chain smoking) a perfect companion for Zuckmayer. As conditions in Europe worsened in the early 1930s, she took a greater interest in his plight, traveled to see him in Henndorf, and offered to help. That she did. During the Atlantic crossing the cable that Zuckmayer received from her was an invitation for his family temporarily to occupy a suite in her spacious New York apartment at 88 Central Park West. American customs officials were notified by her of the family's arrival; and she even arranged to have a letter of welcome, personally signed by President Roosevelt, to be placed in the Zuckmayer file. A happy landing was assured.

On June 6, 1939, coincidentally the birthday of Carl Zuckmayer's mother, they first caught sight of the coast of Long Island and then sailed into the New York harbor: *"Amerika."*[16]

Chapter Four

A FARMHOUSE IN VERMONT

Carl Zuckmayer sat out the Second World War. While Europe experienced a long siege of unprecedented violence and destruction, he withdrew with his family to the quiet and calm of rural New England. As it turned out, they stayed there for over six years, a time that can hardly be described in terms of events and personalities, as had his previous life. Yet it proved to be a significant chapter in his personal biography.

The Zaandam docked not at the Hudson Pier on Manhattan but in Hoboken, New Jersey. An initial foreboding and anxiety in the face of a monstrous New York City was, thanks to Dorothy Thompson, soon dissipated by an easy passage through the American customs. The Zuckmayer clan spent a pleasant fortnight in the princely quarters of Thompson's Central Park apartment, otherwise vacant (except for a helpful Scottish maid), since she was in Hollywood and was no longer living with her current husband, Sinclair Lewis. And they enjoyed the usual tourist attractions: Harlem, China Town, Greenwich Village, Park Avenue, Times Square. After Dorothy Thompson's return, they accompanied her for a visit to her summer home in the hamlet of Barnard, Vermont. The Zuckmayers were deeply impressed by the sprawling landscape—one of America's many scenic wonders, as they eventually learned—which reminded Zuckmayer's wife of the Vienna Woods and him of the Taunus region of Hesse, only many times larger than either. They happened to be in Vermont on the first day of September 1939 when the German army invaded Poland and therewith began the war. In the meanwhile Zuckmayer learned by radio that he was being defamed by the Goebbels press as anti-German, a charge he vigorously denied, though to be sure he was anti-Nazi.

During the initial months in America Zuckmayer shuttled back and forth between New York and Hollywood. In the cinema capital he was entertained by such prominent film directors as Ernst Lubitsch and Fritz Lang, he was put up at the swanky Beverly Hills Hotel, and he was tempted by the offer of a screenplay contract with a steady income. But he quickly concluded: "I won't stay here for long. This is no life for me." He was particularly put off by Los Angeles, "one of the most brutal and ugliest major cities on earth." Finally came an offer to write the script for a Don Juan film starring Errol Flynn. But the idea of devoting his talent to such costumed nonsense revolted him, and he declined, thereby marking the end of his career in Hollywood before it began.[1]

New York City, which initially Zuckmayer had found "grand, wonderful, overwhelming, thrilling," was also losing its luster for him as the almost romantic aura of first impressions began to evaporate. Nonetheless, once more back there in 1940, he managed through Erwin Piscator to gain appointment to a teaching post at the New School for Social Research, where he was assigned to establish a "dramatic workshop" and to conduct a seminar that he called "Humor in Drama," a task for which he was eminently qualified. With some difficulty and much help he learned to formulate thoughts in his still primitive English. As many foreigners like him were currently employed in part-time positions at the New School, Zuckmayer's monthly paycheck was modest, and he was once more plagued by financial problems. He was barely able to rent a cramped apartment that had the compensating virtue of a view out over the Hudson River and the George Washington Bridge. Again he imagined that he was standing above the Rhine. Yet the poverty was proving to be demoralizing, unable as Zuckmayer was to participate in the cultural life of the city or even to afford expensive theaters and cinemas. Worse, Zuckmayer was no more apt to write dramas in New York than he was screenplays in Hollywood.[2]

At the same time there were depressing news reports from Europe. Poland had fallen and was divided between Nazi Germany and Soviet Russia. France seemed paralyzed, Britain isolated. And no reaction was forthcoming from the United States. Meanwhile, with a group of American journalists Dorothy Thompson visited the

Maginot Line in early 1940. Most of her colleagues came away with the conviction that France was "the most secure land in the world." She was not so certain, although she still "continued to believe with all her heart in an allied victory."[3] On May 10 of that year the so-called "phony war" ended with the German invasion of the lowlands and France, followed by Dunkirk and the bombing of London and Coventry. For Zuckmayer and his wife it was all too much. They felt hopeless, scratching out a meager living amidst a strange city and a foreign language. "We had to give up and start anew."[4]

For the Zuckmayers' decision to leave their residence in New York City and to risk relocation at a farm in Vermont, it was of course not coincidental that Dorothy Thompson had a summer home there, which they had already visited twice. Carl Zuckmayer had no experience in farming, but he was willing and indeed eager to learn. And he could obtain financial loans from friends, notably the publisher Alfred Harcourt, to make a start. So it was in the spring of 1941 that the move was made. "We did not have the illusion that this was a path to prosperity, but it appeared as the last and only possibility to continue our lives through free voluntary work," thus sparing the family from "an unworthy and futile existence."[5] They would try to find a home amid green forests and blue lakes, with air clean and fresh, without the bustle and noise of a big city. It might be something like what they had known and loved in Henndorf, only where the winters were colder and the snow deeper. At least the runoff from spring thaws would assure a thick undergrowth of bushes, wild berries aplenty, and apple trees in abundance. Vegetables would flourish despite the hard and rocky soil.

Walking one day that summer in the vicinity of Barnard, Zuckmayer happened on an abandoned farmhouse beside a brook. Built in 1783—medieval times for America, he observed— it was a wooden structure, formed around a large central stone chimney with three fireplaces, located on an imposing tree-filled terrain of 180 acres. There was no electric lighting, only oil lamps. But Zuckmayer met the owner, a Mr. Ward, who asked only fifty dollars a month in rent and promised to fix up the premises to be habitable. It was a deal, and they shook hands on it. Shortly thereafter, the Zuckmayers moved into their primitive new residence.

Europe was now far away. In June 1941 Germany invaded Russia. Most of Carl Zuckmayer's friends were convinced that it was the beginning of the end for the Wehrmacht. Yet, as a decorated military veteran, he initially remained confident that the German general staff had calculated everything. France was conquered, England helpless, America neutral. He therefore expected, alas, a German victory on the eastern front, a notion that caused him much anguish. "The conflict of having to hope for the defeat of my own people, in order to free it from tyranny, filled me with despair." He wanted to see Hitler's humiliation but not a "ruined, downtrodden Germany." The problem, however, would be that it was likely that one was not possible without the other. "I felt myself caught in a contradiction." Hence his undiminished patriotism and his intense hatred of Nazism were irreconcilably at odds.[6]

There was meanwhile the farm to tend. They started by raising chickens, ducks, and geese, then pigs and above all goats, whose milk sold for five times more than that of cows. Zuckmayer adroitly mastered the technique of milking them himself. He also devised an elaborate garden with corn, potatoes, beans, squash, and herbs. He and the children gathered apples from which they made cider and even apple jack, faintly reminding Zuckmayer of French calvados. All of this transpired in the autumn of 1941, a season with colorful splashes of brilliant foliage and extended by Indian summer before ending with fallen leaves.

An indispensable source for the Vermont years is Alice Zuckmayer's charming account entitled *Die Farm in den grünen Bergen*, first published in 1949, seventeen years before Carl Zuckmayer's own memoirs. She aptly portrayed both the pleasures and hardships of their new life. With no relevant experience or family tradition, they "had to learn again to see, hear, touch, smell, taste . . ."[7] More detailed about their daily routines than her husband, Alice precisely noted that they started with 57 chickens, 20 ducks, 5 geese, 4 goats, 2 pigs, 2 dogs, 3 cats. And that was merely the beginning. The Zuckmayers shared the necessary chores of tending the house, the garden, and the menagerie of animals. Each had specialties. Zuck was better at milking goats, and he assumed responsibility for bringing in wood to heat their quarters during the winter months, which meant arising at 3 a.m. every morning to fill the stove with sticks of wood that he had previously chopped, sawed, and stacked. Alice did the household cleaning and, in the absence of a sewing machine, expertly handled the mounting of curtains and the repair of clothing. They even struck a "gentleman's agreement": he took care of breakfast, whereas Alice cooked the other meals, not exactly a 50/50 arrangement.

This was all very well, and even in some regards romantic. They were assured of a comfortable if extremely strenuous existence that would, so they imagined, provide Zuck the circumstances to continue his work as a playwright. At first, however, it was not so. He seemed somewhat befuddled and out of sorts. "He had lost his touch and resonance," Alice remarked, and was capable only of producing "abstractions and vagaries" that ended up in a drawer. Among them was a novel about a character named Lencher Demuth. In January 1942 he concluded that his work "was all wasted and lost, [and] now myself, my language, my fantasy, and my soul." But he then read a part of his manuscript to his wife, who offered encouragement; and consequently, so he wrote, "I believe it will be quite a special book—above all very humorous." He expected to finish it that spring, but at the end of March he abandoned it again. He did manage to compose a few essays and even some poetry, but those were hardly the ingredients of a stellar career to which he had once been accustomed.[8]

Although she scarcely mentioned it in her otherwise observant narrative, Alice noticed that her husband began to withdraw to his room in the evening. We know now what was on his mind. In 1943 he was preparing the initial sketches of what proved to be his most serious and profound drama, *Des Teufels General,* which he finished—"in an inexplicable way," Alice recorded—during their final three years on the Vermont farm. Hence, with his latest manuscript already in hand, Carl Zuckmayer would be ready for postwar Europe.[9]

In his memoirs, Zuckmayer added some missing details, beginning in 1941. It had snowed heavily on the wintry morning of December 7. The Zuckmayers were therefore snowbound when they heard the news of Pearl Harbor. President Roosevelt promptly declared war on Japan, and Germany was sure to follow. As Germans, how would their family be dealt with? At the general store Zuckmayer discovered there was no change, because Vermonters did not speak of the war. But it was necessary to register as "enemy aliens." Accordingly, Zuckmayer received a visit from the local sheriff to whom he explained his flight from the Nazis. Everything was in order, he was told, only there should be no shortwave radio receivers, cameras, or weapons in the farmhouse, nor were trips of more than twenty miles allowed without official permission. [10]

There was much activity around Barnard when Dorothy Thompson arrived for the summer: lots of visitors at her estate, invitations, guests, parties, and gallons of whiskey. Otherwise all was quiet, so that the Zuckmayers hardly saw other people for weeks and months at a time. Apart from his farming chores, he devoted the springtime to sawing and stacking wood so that it could dry out over the summer. Years went by at this slow pace. Naturally, given the time of war, a certain anti-German sentiment was prevalent— rather, Zuckmayer thought, like anti-Semitism. But he himself was not the object of it. "The Americans had understanding and respect for refugees and exiles who supported the good elements in their people." In a letter to an immigrant friend he expanded on this theme: "Personally, my attitude toward America is entirely positive, and I hate the people who are constantly criticizing the Americans because they are in many ways 'different' from us. I believe that, among Americans, the heart is sound—I could hardly say anything more positive."[11]

In early 1943, for the first time, Zuckmayer left his Vermont abode and ventured to New York City to celebrate Max Reinhardt's seventieth birthday. He returned a few weeks later to attend his funeral. There he again met Erich Maria Remarque, and he also encountered the famous German anti-war painter, George Gross, now a professor at the New York Art Students League, who seemed quite American, although, even more than Zuckmayer, he suffered from his exile and had become an alcoholic. Disturbingly, reports arrived that the central railway station in Mainz had been bombed. Zuckmayer's parents lived only five minutes away, and there was no way to tell whether they had survived (a second allied bombing in 1945 would destroy nearly the entire town). Yet by the end of November 1942, after the allied landing in North Africa, he found reason to believe that "the events of the last few weeks have brought a turning point in this war, so that we can hope for a good ending and perhaps also once more a reunion alive and well."[12]

After several years of silence he began writing again just as the decisive battle of Stalingrad hung in the balance. The new play was inspired by, but not based upon, the ill-fated demise of his old friend Ernst Udet, an air force officer whom he had last seen in Berlin in 1936 and who was killed in a plane accident in December 1941. With an opening burst Zuckmayer wrote out the entire first act in three weeks and then left it untouched, but it took him the next two years to complete the rest: "I lived with the play, I lived with Germany." In truth, the drama was highly autobiographical, expressing Zuckmayer's own love of his country and the anguish of determining how far a patriot like him could go in opposing it. The same theme occurred in Zuckmayer's speech at a memorial service in New York for his old friend, Carlo Mierendorff, in March 1944, which he closed by swearing *"always to stand up for the German people."*[13]

It is noteworthy that, at nearly the same time as Carl Zuckmayer was beginning in 1943 to write *Des Teufels General,* he also started the composition of a so-called "secret report" for the American Office of Strategic Services. Exactly how and why he was commissioned by the OSS—predecessor of the postwar CIA—to undertake this task is not clear. Apparently the formidable immigrant historians Hajo Holborn and Felix Gilbert, themselves refugees from Nazi Germany, were involved. But the main credit probably belongs to their modest colleague Emmy Rado, who was in direct contact about the matter with Zuckmayer.[14]

The idea was to survey the cast of German and Austrian personalities in theater and film who had remained in their native land after the Nazi seizure of power. His report demonstrated that Zuckmayer was little given to sweeping generalizations or minute analysis of them. Rather, he chose to present almost 150 individual portraits of authors, directors, and actors about whom he could offer personal observations. He did venture that "most actors tend to a kind of infantilism," and that "many actors show clear signs of schizophrenia." But most of them, he added, did not become Nazis— not even Gustaf Gründgens, perhaps the most notorious example of the stage and film performers who profited from patronage by the Hitler regime.[15] After some dithering Zuckmayer settled on four categories, and he did not hesitate to name the names of those who belonged to each: positive, negative, a mixture of positive and negative, plus a nebulous fourth rubric of the politically indifferent. Among the ones whom Zuckmayer judged positively as publishers and authors, he especially singled out Peter Suhrkamp, Richard Weichert, and Ernst Barlach. Also receiving honorable mention were the actors Käthe Dorsch (with whom he was rumored to have had an affair) and Heinz Rühmann (who had a Jewish spouse and later became a star in the postwar film version of *Der Hauptmann von Köpenick)*. Zuckmayer did not stint in his praise of these courageous dissenters, as for example when lauding Rühmann's "impeccable character and his really bewitching personality."[16]

Quite the opposite was in store for the negative figures, which notably included Hans Reimann and Gottfried Benn. About the former, Zuckmayer simply remarked: "Of the Nazi creatures, Hans Reimann is the most evil example."[17] And one of Benn's literary efforts was caustically dismissed by Zuckmayer: "There is nothing more awful."[18]

A handful of outstanding individuals were relegated by Zuckmayer to a negative subset of "special cases": Friedrich Sieburg, the popular author of non-fiction volumes like *Gott in Frankreich*; and the brilliant director of documentary films such as *Triumph des Willens*, Leni Riefenstahl, whom Zuckmayer unflatteringly characterized as a "severely hysterical person—boundlessly ambitious." Here, Zuckmayer did not shy from a bit of gossip: Riefenstahl was said to be of Jewish origin ("could be") and to have slept with Hitler (unlikely because of "assumed mutual impotence").[19]

Zuckmayer was less categorical about the third category, whose representatives displayed both complexity and ambiguity after 1933. Besides Gründgens, this list included Ernst Jünger and his brother Friedrich Georg Jünger; the ne plus ultra conductor of the Berlin Philharmonic, Wilhelm Furtwängler; the celebrated film actor Emil Jannings (co-star with Marlene Dietrich in *Der Blaue Engel)*; and the internationally acclaimed film director G. W. Pabst, about whom Zuckmayer rather cattily remarked: "Actually, I don't like him, since he laughs so loud and so often *with his mouth—and never with his eyes*."[20]

Surely this abbreviated summary is sufficient to suggest the personal tone and non-theoretical nature of Zuckmayer's *Geheimreport* for the OSS. What practical use was ever made of his kaleidoscopic rendition is impossible to say. As a minimum, we may conclude that the report at least revealed the broad scope of Zuckmayer's friends and acquaintances as well as his alertness to the impact of German fascism on the stage and screen of his homeland in the 1930s.

Once the struggle at Stalingrad was decided in early 1943, the inevitable events leading to German defeat cascaded one after the other. The assassination attempt against Hitler on July 20, 1944, fell into that context, as did the allied landing in France and the rumors of a German capitulation in the early spring of 1945. Or had Hitler merely retreated to an Alpine fortress? Uncertainties abounded, among them whether Zuckmayer's parents were still alive. That phase closed with the end of the war in May 1945, the confirmed reports of Hitler's death, and a terse cable: "Parents alive."[21] So now, the question was posed of how and when Carl Zuckmayer might return to Europe.

Chapter Five

THE RETURN TO EUROPE

In the immediate postwar period it was extremely difficult to reach occupied Germany and Austria from the United States except for military personnel. There was no regular cross-Atlantic civilian travel, and even sending letters and packages was at first forbidden. Furthermore, as usual, Carl Zuckmayer was nearly bereft of finances. In the late summer of 1946, as a consequence, he was still farming in Vermont.

However, Zuckmayer and his wife had been granted American citizenship, and he was now free to apply for a post in the federal government with hopes of being returned to Germany on a cultural mission of some sort. After a tedious and protracted tussle with the bureaucracy he received such an appointment. While his wife stayed in Vermont, and with Winnetou off to the University of California, Zuckmayer's first stop was New York City, where he briefly occupied a small office on Madison Avenue in the heart of Manhattan. His job was ostensibly to analyze reports from American occupation authorities about cultural activity in German cities, an employment that he found to be fairly useless. Nor was he pleased to be back in the big city, solidifying his satisfaction that he had lived out the war years on a Vermont farm.

Next, Zuckmayer was transferred to Washington, D.C., where he took up duties in the Ministry of War at the Pentagon—an intimidating labyrinth of hallways and offices, as he observed, that might well serve as the setting for a Fritz Lang fantasy film. Finally he received travel orders to visit major cities in Germany in order to evaluate the cultural activity there and to make recommendations to improve it. Although his mission was under military aegis, he was allowed to maintain his civilian status and not required to wear a uniform. Zuckmayer carried with him a specific official assignment: to write a report for the American Department of War on conditions in central Europe, especially—once again—the theater and film activity, which he was particularly qualified to judge. Along with his memoirs (in part based on it), this document remains one of the most clear-sighted and correct evaluations of Germany in the immediate postwar era. It conveyed his frank appraisal gathered during his stay on the European continent of 125 days from November 4, 1946, to March 30, 1947.[1]

Leaving his wife on the Vermont farm, to which he bade an emotional farewell, Zuckmayer caught a night flight to Europe. His plane landed briefly for refueling in Paris, then made a longer stop at the Rhein-Main airport. On that evening Zuckmayer had his first view of massive ruins as he walked through the streets of Frankfurt. And for the first time in years he heard pedestrians speaking in his native Rhenish dialect. But "I felt much like a foreigner," he confessed.[2] Then he was transported on a military aircraft to the Berlin-Tempelhof airport, where he boarded a bus. The drive into the city was eerily depressing, as Berlin was barely recognizable. Along the way the Tiergarten was empty and flat, literally shaven by the many Berliners who had chopped down trees for firewood. The neighborhoods of Grunewald, Lichterfelde, and Dahlem appeared more normal, since they had been largely spared from heavy bombing by the allies in the expectation of locating their headquarters in the city's West End. Yet even there citizens were to suffer from the extreme cold of the coming winter when, due to a lack of adequate heating in homes and apartments, frozen pipes forced them to stand in long lines seeking water. In November 1946 Zuckmayer paused on a corner beside the "grotesque ruins" of the Memorial Church (*Gedächtniskirche*), a sobering fragment of its former self, where the once elegant Tauentzienstrasse meets the Kurfürstendamm near the Bahnhof Zoo, a site that had always been brilliantly lighted at dusk in the Weimar years and now stood dark and quiet. Nearby the famous old Berlin department store, Kaufhaus des Westens, was burned out. This is what was left of the city that had earlier been the hub of European civilization.[3]

Zuckmayer met his youthful flame Annemarie Seidel. "Mirl" was now married to the publisher Peter Suhrkamp. She was exceedingly slender and pale. Her husband was frail and ill after excruciating months in a Nazi concentration camp. They spent the evening with Zuckmayer emptying two bottles, one whisky and the other cognac, that he had brought in his baggage from America. The occasion was brightened for him by his first telephone contact with his parents. Decidedly, he was back in Germany. But was he still a German?[4]

Zuckmayer moved on westward to Darmstadt, just south of Frankfurt, and then to the ruins of Mainz. He found the remains of his parents' former home near the totally devastated main train station, but he was unable to recognize the pathway that he had once taken from there to school. He continued to Stuttgart (where he met the future president of the Bonn Republic, Theodor Heuss), to Ulm, and to Munich. Badly damaged, the Bavarian capital seemed "dreary" and "depressing." Its inhabitants were "dirty, morose, and bitter." Zuckmayer was struck by the overcrowded train stations he was seeing and by the many cripples in the streets. Munich also triggered unpleasant memories of the Nazi past: "We knew that the murderers were still among us." At last he arrived at the town of Oberstdorf to find his parents alive but older. Their survival had a special meaning for Carl Zuckmayer: *"I did not need to hate."* That sentiment was reinforced when he learned that a Nazi official had protected his mother after 1933 by surreptitiously hiding her papers and birth certificate.[5]

Zuckmayer traveled to Heidelberg, still "intact," the only German town of its size not destroyed by allied bombing. He also visited Wiesbaden and Tübingen in Germany; and, after Munich, finally Salzburg, Linz, and Vienna in Austria. Along the way he found time to collect his thoughts. He was skeptical about the American program of denazification, because Germany had undergone no inner revolution. Not gradual reform but a complete change was necessary. At the same time he did not believe there was any danger of a return to Nazism. "For the Germany of 1945 National Socialism was doubtless finished."[6] He was therefore hopeful for the future of German youth who were currently living in a "positive vacuum." And as it turned out, he was prescient about what would eventually fill that void— in a word, Europe.[7] Understandably, Zuckmayer also had moments of introspection. Where did he belong, and what was his primary allegiance as a citizen? At a hastily organized press conference, he was asked those questions. His answer was: "Write that I am an American and will remain so." In a 1947 article in the Berlin *Tagesspiegel*, however, he had to admit that "my German is still better than my English." For the time being, in truth, the matter remained unresolved.[8]

In general Zuckmayer found contacts with the German citizenry in the American zone of occupation to be disappointing and insufficient. "We don't reach the people. We find no way into their heads and hearts."[9] The one great exception was support for the performing arts, especially in the American sector of Berlin, where he saw "a chance for a new orientation and a moral renewal."[10] Zuckmayer estimated that fully twenty percent of the capital's public regularly attended the theater. Berlin already had two operas and twelve functioning theater ensembles, and "the theaters are everywhere filled."[11] Moreover, the level of stage performances was "surprisingly high," given that sixty percent of all theaters in the American zone had been completely destroyed.[12]

Zuckmayer paid far less attention to the film industry. Shattered by the war, the production of German film studios did not resume until March 1947. Consequently the public initially had to be content with a few synchronized or subtitled American sagas from Hollywood. The most popular were *The Keys of the Kingdom*, starring Gregory Peck as a troubled Scottish Catholic priest; Otto Preminger's mysterious romance *Laura,* with Gene Tierney; and a touching comedy, *The Shop Around the Corner*, directed by Ernst Lubitsch. Zuckmayer made little effort to look further, and the most he could find to say about the film industry in Vienna was that it displayed "hopeless confusion."[13]

In addition to his official duties, Zuckmayer also took advantage of the opportunity to seek out old friends and to make new acquaintances. Of particular interest to him were the relatives and still living representatives of the German resistance movement. Among those families whom he contacted were such now honored names as Moltke, Hassell, Stauffenberg, Gerstenmaier, Schlabrendorff, Sophie and Hans Scholl. It would be many years before their story was adequately told. But already Zuckmayer was obviously aware that the sacrifice of such German heroes deserved to be remembered as an integral part of Germany's past experience and future recovery.[14]

With the script for *Des Teufels General* conveniently prepared, it did not take Zuckmayer long after the war to reestablish his reputation. As things stood, Zürich was the largest undamaged and free theater in German-speaking Central Europe. It was there that Zuckmayer had in 1938 enjoyed his last premier, *Bellman,* and his new play was now scheduled to debut in December 1946. Travel restrictions were such that he had no permission to enter Switzerland, but he managed secretly to catch an "illegal" auto ride across the border. He thereby experienced his moment of renewed triumph in a large, unscathed, and prosperous Germanic city that was full of light and unimpeded traffic. Afterwards he returned to celebrate the New Year with his parents. With him he brought a notion of the possibility that perhaps Switzerland would be the solution to his most urgent concern.

Zuckmayer was aware that he was not an American, even though he still owned a home in Vermont and carried a U.S. passport. Yet at the same time "we were no longer really at home in Germany." In truth, he belonged neither to the victors nor to the vanquished.[15]

By following Zuckmayer's correspondence in the decade or so after the Second World War, one can gather a clear notion of his intense emotional struggle to determine where in the world he belonged. He realized early on, while in Vermont, that remaining in the United States was not a viable option, because his reputation, talent, and linguistic excellence were so firmly planted in Europe. To an Austrian friend he confided in 1945: "The emphasis of my work will always lie in the German language area, and I remain—with all my gratitude, loyalty, and love for America—what I am." Tellingly, he added that in recent years he had spoken English by day but dreamed in German at night.[16]

Three years later, writing in English, he confirmed that judgment: "In my native language I'm an imaginative, creative, inspired writer. I could be none of that in English."[17]

By the late 1950s the issue had essentially been decided. "In the long run," he wrote to another friend in Paris, "I can no longer manage a double existence between two continents and will doubtless sink roots again in Europe with a home in Switzerland."[18]

At the same time he suffered pangs of regret. To an American acquaintance he wrote back: "I can still say *our* country," but even if the "halfwits" on Broadway were to produce Zuckmayer's plays now, "I still would not belong to American litterature [*sic*] but to German poetry and European theater." Admittedly, nevertheless, giving up his American citizenship "leaves a wound in my heart." And he confessed: "Sometimes, I feel a sharp sting of homesickness—sometimes a sweet dream-like nostalgia—for my lost country: Vermont."[19]

All of which still left open the issue of exactly where the Zuckmayers would settle. Although Zuck considered a return to the ransacked and ruined mill in Henndorf out of the question, in 1958 he did apply for Austrian citizenship. As he explained to the American consulate in Salzburg: "Since my litterary [*sic*] work, which is deeply rooted in European mentality and tradition, gives me no chance to make a living in the United States, I decided to take personal residence in Europe." He promised therefore to return his U.S. passport as soon as he received an Austrian one.[20]

Finally the choice fell on Saas-Fee, a tiny village high in the Swiss Alps, which the Zuckmayer couple had discovered in 1938, four months before their flight from Europe. He explained that decision to another correspondent in Berlin. It was not for political reasons that they did not choose to dwell in the postwar *Bundesrepublik* of Germany. Indeed, he and his wife might have preferred to take up residence there "if Berlin were still what it once was," since "it is still the only large city in the German language area that has an attraction for me."[21]

Obviously that attraction was related to the considerable success Zuckmayer was enjoying in the revived German theater scene during the first years after 1945, notably with repeated productions of *Der Hauptmann von Köpenick* and *Des Teufels General*. But he soon learned that with success came stress. Well received by the Swiss press, *Des Teufels General* was acclaimed in Switzerland. But how would it be received in Germany? The answer appeared with a Frankfurt production of the play in November 1947: it was controversial. German audiences were moved and impressed that Zuckmayer had come so close to an accurate portrayal of the dilemmas that had been faced by those who dared to take action against Hitler's regime, risking as they did the accusation that, by doing so, they were betraying their own fatherland. Were they really heroes or just traitors? Many found it difficult to grasp that this painful contemporary drama could have been written abroad in America by someone who had not actually experienced the war at first hand—whereas Zuckmayer himself contended that his story could only have been conceived from a distance, not in the midst of all the horrors that had roiled Germany since 1933. Heated discussions ensued until, during a lecture tour in the Rhineland near the end of 1948, Zuckmayer suffered a heart attack. Still in his early fifties, he was able to recover while recuperating at a sanatorium in Oberstdorf, where he was daily attended by his widowed mother.

Once released, Zuckmayer longed to resume his normal pace of life. Yet taking refuge in the magnificent Alpine surroundings of Saas-Fee was a far more rational option. He remembered the first time he and Alice had climbed 1600 meters above a base station to the village they would come to call home. There was no road traffic at that time, only a pilgrimage path with fourteen small stone chapels along the way. Reaching the top, they looked out over the mountains and one of them sighed: "Here. . . If we could remain here." Indeed they did. Carl and Alice Zuckmayer lived in Saas-Fee from July 1958 to 1977, when he died, formerly a German, not quite American, Austrian, or Swiss, and yet as ever a European and a citizen of the world.[23]

The schoolboy, about 1908

The soldier, 1914-1918

The young playwright

At his desk, 1930

With his guitar, 1939

With Alice in Vermont, 1939-1946

The gentleman farmer, 1939-1946

With a cigar, 1959

The bon vivant, 1960s

With a pipe, 1963

In his study, about 1970

The successful playwright

At the window in Saas-Fee, 1970s

In the Swiss Alps, 1970s

Der fröhliche Weinberg

Schinderhannes

Der Hauptmann von Köpenick

Des Teufels General

PART TWO

THE AUTHOR

Chapter Six

FAILURE AND SUCCESS

Finally it is by his plays that Carl Zuckmayer must be judged as a writer. True, he tried his hand at numerous other forms of prose: essays, novels, short stories, journalistic sketches, and so forth. Frequently he also composed poetry.[1] Yet his reputation and his self-esteem both depended primarily on his dramatic inventions. Never mind that two of his longest works—an interminable pastoral novel, unpromisingly entitled *Salvare oder die Magdalena von Bozen,* and his autobiography, *Als wär's ein Stück von mir*—were not meant for the stage. Nonetheless, Zuckmayer's personal and financial fortunes always derived from his failure or success as a playwright.

It cannot be the purpose of this relatively short appreciation of Zuckmayer's writings to recreate the plot and to evaluate every one of his theatrical efforts. Instead, it is well to confine ourselves to his most significant literary creations. These should be sufficient to draw out the salient aspects of Zuckmayer's stage productions and enable us to locate him among the most notable writers in Central Europe during the early twentieth century.

Kreuzweg (possibly translated either as *Crossroads* or *The Way of the Cross*), completed and first performed in 1920, was Zuckmayer's maiden effort as a playwright; and it was a total flop. Reading through his misbegotten piece nearly a century after its inception, one can well understand the thoroughly negative public reaction and the merciless opprobrium of Berlin critics like Alfred Kerr. Even before the first scene opens, a note appended to the printed version offers a telling explanation: "This play has no historical background"—nor, the author might have added, comprehensible plot. Ostensibly the setting is during the early sixteenth-century German Peasants' War, but that context is not explained and lacks any particular relevance. More than one of Zuckmayer's biographers have noted a much more proximate relationship with the revolutionary events of 1918-1919, which immediately followed Germany's defeat in the First World War and marked the founding of the Weimar Republic. Yet there is no surrogate for Karl Liebknecht or Rosa Luxemburg, no Communist Party, and no parallel to the concluding brutal conquest of Munich by Freekorps militia troops or the flight of a Kaiser from Berlin.

Instead, the audience must endure pretentious dialogue, sometimes in rhyming couplets, as if it were a rather inept translation of Shakespeare, full of sound and fury, signifying very little. The characters, except for the young female lead Christa (embodied in the Berlin premier by Zuckmayer's newly found intimate friend Annemarie Seidel), remain ill-defined. They do not speak; they declaim. When there is a possible interaction between persons, they often seem to talk right by one another. Emotions are suggested but left hanging in the general confusion. Several individuals appear, speak a few lines, then disappear. If there is an identifiable central constellation of them, it is provided by the triangle of the father Christian Kutter, his daughter Christa, and her suitors. But any such potential coherence is undercut by a bothersome structural problem: this relatively short drama is divided into four acts that are presented in a total of twenty different scenes—whereby it is usually unclear what one scene has to do with the next. It is all very perplexing and little edifying. At last the end comes with Christa's unsung death. Curtain.

A few months before the opening of *Kreuzweg* in December 1920, Zuckmayer had high hopes for his debut in Berlin: "it is my first good, and *I firmly believe,* most accomplished effort. I believe that *here* I am in my proper and legitimate place."[3] As he later explained, he was not strongly influenced by the drama of Expressionism but rather by the new wave of painting (Franz Marc, Chagall, Kokoschka), by contemporary music (Debussy, Stravinsky, Schönberg, Hindemith), and also by dramatists such as Paul Claudel.[4] Yet he was forced to admit that his firstborn play was a humiliating defeat, especially when *Kreuzweg* closed only two nights after its premier. Looking back as an elderly man, he was able to philosophize about that disappointment, referring to it as "a necessary experience" that was actually "better than a success would have been then."[5] However dubious that claim may be in retrospect, one thing was clear in the 1920s: Carl Zuckmayer would never gain public recognition or survive as a playwright unless he changed his style.

Der fröhliche Weinberg was Carl Zuckmayer's first triumph as a playwright. It premiered almost simultaneously in Berlin and Frankfurt shortly before Christmas 1925, two years after major financial reforms had set Germany on a renewed path to prosperity. To say that the national mood was celebratory might be a bit much, but certainly the worst days of the postwar era now seemed to belong to the past; and the theater-going public was prepared to greet Zuckmayer's farce with unrestrained peals of laughter.

Act One sets the location of the play and immediately plunges its main characters into a ticklish situation. An elderly local Rhineland vintner, Jean Baptiste Gunderloch, wants to divest himself of his holdings. He plans to auction half of his vineyard and extensive wine cellar while bestowing the remainder on his adopted and now engaged daughter Klärchen as a wedding gift. There are only two conditions: she must be pregnant, and gladly so. With a certain bravado her fiancé Knuzius reassures the father: "It will be done, Herrr Gunderloch, it will be done."[6] Gunderloch has another problem. As a widower he does not want to become a burden to his family. He also needs a female companion: "Being alone, that is nothing." Ideally he would fancy a young beauty. But he fears none of them will have him.[7] Now appears the major complication. Speaking to her younger sister Babette, Klärchen confesses that all is not well with her engagement. Why, then, did she take up with Knuzius? Klärchen explains simply that he gave her a strong drink, and "then it happened."[8] Furthermore she shares a secret with Babette: Klärchen is sweet on Jochen Most, young captain of a small ship that plies the Rhine. The two meet, flirt, embrace, and pledge their mutual affection. But at that point Jochen's sister Annemarie inconveniently reveals to all concerned that Klärchen and Knuzius are engaged. Just before the curtain falls on Act One, Klärchen whispers something into Knuzius' ear. The audience can only assume that she has told him of her pregnancy.

Act Two brings relief from this dramatic tension. It is played out in a pub, one of Zuckmayer's favorite settings, where there is much drinking, boisterous singing, and loud drunken conversations. As the alcohol flows more freely the milling crowd becomes chaotic and the scene grows uglier. Banter turns to brawling. Knuzius and Jochen become involved, exchanging fierce looks and then blows. Suddenly the tone is serious, and Jochen is heard to utter: "No pardon. Life or death!" Zuckmayer adds a stage direction: "Outside the skirmish continues."[9]

Act Three presents a predictable happy ending. First of all, Gunderloch and Annemarie are united (Zuckmayer knew something about courting an Annemarie). After they first kiss Gunderloch urges a quick consummation of their newly discovered romance. Annemarie attempts to resist, but he carries her into the garden where they abandon any ambiguity.[10]

Meanwhile, Knuzius has begun to pursue Babette in his own uncouth manner, grabbing her bottom (Zuckmayer is charmingly explicit about her *"Popo,"* a common German euphemism) and declaring his love. Babette resists, reminding him that he is still engaged to her elder sister. He of course claims not to care about those vows and renews his advances. What comes of this encounter, if anything, is unclear and left as a matter of lesser importance. At last the third pair of lovers—with much hugging and kissing—can realize their dreams. The solution of their dilemma with Knuzius is realized with ridiculous ease: Klärchen confesses that the profession of her pregnancy was a lie. So the sun comes up. The roosters crow. As dawn breaks everyone arises except Knuzius, still asleep and snoring on a pile of manure. Gunderloch and Annemarie gather with Jochen and Klärchen. The four rejoice and share a hearty laugh at Knuzius as he awakens. Yet it is Knuzius, in effect, who has the final word: "It was only a joke!"[11]

This brief synopsis is sufficient evidence that Carl Zuckmayer had in fact reinvented himself as a playwright. He had decisively modified his style in three identifiable regards. First, the new play put great emphasis on a specific time and place. The setting is the autumn of 1921 in Rhenish wine country during the harvest season. The plot, such as it is, was of relatively little consequence and indeed might be considered something of a banality. What counts is not so much a story line but a slice of life presented in realistic and believable terms. This first factor was reinforced by a second. The play was written entirely in Zuckmayer's native Hessian dialect. Its characters do not declaim, as in *Kreuzweg,* but speak in an ordinary patois of the Rhineland. In his ability to recreate such appropriate and carefully observed speech patterns, Zuckmayer had no peer among German playwrights of his time. Third, accordingly, he was thereby able to conjure a comic atmosphere that sustained an intimate personal interaction of the principal actors. The stage thus became the scene of sharply defined and nuanced relationships that elicited a positive and indeed delighted response from German audiences—and even from several of Zuckmayer's formerly hostile critics. And Carl Zuckmayer was fully conscious of his newly won importance. *Der fröhliche Weinberg* was unquestionably "an outstanding success," he wrote, "which suddenly made theater history" and "finished off the abstract pathetic Expressionism" of that time.[12] The indigent fledgling playwright of the early 1920s had thus become by mid-decade a celebrated theatrical phenomenon throughout Central Europe.

Less than two years after Carl Zuckmayer's unanticipated emergence as one of the major figures of the German stage another of his dramas premiered at the Lessing Theater in Berlin. At first glance this new play, entitled *Schinderhannes,* appeared to continue the recently deployed successful literary formula of *Der fröhliche Weinberg:* a specific era and geographic location, a generous serving of folksy Rhenish dialect, and a tightly focused scenario that permitted the principal characters to emote and interact in a realistic manner. Despite the play's chronological setting during the Napoleonic wars at the outset of the nineteenth century—which, according to Zuckmayer's stage instructions, should not be emphasized by the mise en scène— the entire production was meant to have a contemporary effect that clearly evoked the postwar years of the Weimar Republic. This time the action takes place in the Hunsrück, a hilly and heavily wooded area southwest of Mainz, whence the Nahe River descends into the Rhine. Here a legendary Germanic Robin Hood, Johann Bückler alias Schinderhannes, roams the territory while robbing the rich to give to the poor and using whatever violent means are necessary to thwart the French occupation. For all his swagger and insurrectionary demeanor, however, Bückler also displays a tender and sensitive personal side in his courtship of the young and innocent Julchen Blasius.

Unlike *Der fröhliche Weinberg,* however, this romantic involvement is swiftly resolved in Act One. Hence the audience is exposed without delay to love scenes that remain among the most touching passages in Zuckmayer's entire repertoire. The language becomes simple and limpid as Julchen readily accepts Bückler's advances. Therewith, right from the beginning, their liaison has already been decided, and a young police officer named Adam has no chance in his pursuit of Julchen. Rather, as she confides to her sister Margaret, she wishes to stay with her new lover forever.[13] At his next effort to promote a romantic bond with Julchen, Adam accordingly receives a dismissive cold shoulder. With unadorned prose Zuckmayer thus makes it early apparent that *Schinderhannes* will not merely repeat the comic intrigues of *Der fröhliche Weinberg* and that he has altogether different intentions in mind, which are to be unraveled in the three acts that follow.

Act Two seems unduly long and could doubtless have benefited from some pruning. A year has passed since Bückler and Julchen became a couple. As often in a Zuckmayer drama, the scene is a pub,*"Grüner Baum,"* which is animated by coarse talk and accordion music. It is the evening of Easter Saturday. No one knows where Bückler is—until he finally shows up, laughing, with Julchen at his side. He is informed that French troops have invested the Hunsrück. Soon he meets and converses with a couple of French officers who tell of their mission to cleanse the territory of roaming bandits. Unaware of Bückler's identity, they also disclose that a bounty of 5000 gulden has been offered for the arrest of Schinderhannes, dead or alive, and that his supporters have all been condemned to death. After returning to his friends, Bückler boasts that he is undeterred. He and his band will fight on and rid the land of foreigners. When the others depart, he and Julchen are left alone. She pleads with him to abandon the struggle and to hide. He refuses: "There is no turning back. I can do it. Because I must. And will." [14] That utterance provokes the first serious argument between the two. Julchen again begs him to flee to safety. She adds that she has no regrets and pledges to follow him wherever he wants. When Julchen then attempts to end the dispute and step outside, Bückler angrily blocks the door and throws her down. Without a word, she arises, dons her cloak, and exits. [15]

The brief Act Three takes place at a village in the high country of the Hunsrück. There a military recruiter is attempting to enlist volunteers for "the German Kaiser's glorious army."[16] Why they should choose to die for Prussia is not evident to most of the onlookers, and they scatter. Bückler arrives and remarks that they could do worse than join the army. Before he can act on that premise, a pale and disheveled Margaret enters and announces to Bückler that Julchen has delivered a baby. Bückler leaves and finds his lover in a cornfield, clutching the child to her bosom. He reacts with delighted surprise, almost beyond expression, managing only to exclaim: "It lives! It has hands and feet."[17] Then a crucial episode concludes Act Three. At a barracks of the Kaiser's army on the Rhine's Right Bank, where Bückler and a few of his supporters have presented themselves, they agree to join against the French. For an instant their induction procedure is played for comedy. Hilariously, each of them claims to be named Heinrich Schmitt, including Bückler. But the commotion turns dark when his true identity is revealed. He is arrested and placed in handcuffs.

The staging of Act Four is divided into three very short but separate scenes. The first occurs at a wooden tower in Mainz that serves as a prison. There in Julchen's cell she is told by a chaplain that her baby will be returned to her and that she will be released on the next day. She asks about Bückler: will he soon be set free, or must he sit under arrest for a few years? The chaplain reluctantly admits that Schinderhannes and nineteen of his followers have already been sentenced to death. Crestfallen, Julchen recognizes that the situation is hopeless. A second scene transpires at dawn before the gates of Mainz, the site of execution, where a noisy crowd has gathered. Gaiety prevails. Children sing the *"Lied vom Schinderhannes."* A few passing French soldiers are also heard singing *"Auprès de ma blonde."* The church bells of Mainz ring in the distance. But suddenly attention switches back to Julchen's cell in the wooden tower, the ultimate third scene. With bayonets drawn, guards seize Bückler, to whom Julchen quickly says adieu. He and his band of fellow rebels are led out to the gallows. Zuckmayer's script spares the audience from a sight of the execution. But there can be no mistake about the outcome: Schinderhannes is gone.[18]

If this play, albeit often performed, proved to be less of a sensation than *Der fröhliche Weinberg,* it nonetheless displayed

Zuckmayer as a confident author marshaling some of the elements that had made him a success. Again one finds the rich dialogue, the attention to a certain locale, the perceptively drawn personalities, the comedic excursions. True, these traits were eventually crowded out by a macabre ending, the inevitable tragedy of a legend too familiar to be basically tampered with. Julchen must poignantly suffer, and Johann Bückler must bravely face death. Although not quite a box office hit, Zuckmayer's skillful version of the absorbing Schinderhannes tale did nothing to dim the luster of his vaulting career as a German playwright.

It has often been said, here and elsewhere, that Carl Zuckmayer was as a playwright less invested in constructing a plot than in creating an atmosphere. In none of his major stage productions was that tendency so pronounced as *Katharina Knie,* which also debuted at Berlin's Lessing Theater barely a year after *Schinderhannes,* that is, four days before Christmas 1928.

Once again the setting is in the Rhineland, this time in the Palatinate *(Rheinpfalz)* at the market square of a small town where the traveling troupe of Carl Knie (always called "Father Knie") is set up to perform its high-wire act, much in the spirit and with the trappings of an itinerant circus. The widower Knie has with him his three children: twenty-four year old Katharina and two sons, Fritz and Lorenz, also in their twenties. Among the other performers is notably Ignaz Scheel, a muscular young trampoline artist who curiously bears the nickname "the beautiful Nazi." That moniker, deserved or not, at least serves to fix the time of the play's first two acts in 1923, when Adolf Hitler first made his dubious public reputation. But Nazism has no part in the proceedings, although the rampant inflation of that year does. A seat at Knie's makeshift arena, for instance, costs 750 marks, a bargain at the time compared to a cinema, where one might have to pay double that amount to enter.[19]

The story that unfolds may be quickly outlined. In Act One a wealthy landowner of the region named Martin Rothacker appears with two police officers to investigate the robbery of three sacks of oats from his estate. After a long discussion, Katharina confesses that she was the thief and claims that she alone is guilty. The as yet unanswerable question is why. Rothacker refuses to press charges against her and disappears. The troupe goes back to work. Then Act Two supplies the missing answer. Although it is early morning, Katharina is dressed up. She announces that she has just returned the oats. When asked why she put on fine clothing to do so, she immediately responds that she might have met someone along the way. Clearly that someone is Rothacker, who promptly shows up with two helpers to bring back the three full sacks of oats. Katharina resists his offer, he insists, and their flirtation begins. Rothacker also chats with Father Knie, who worries about keeping his daughter with the troupe. Maybe he should send her away in search of a better life? Rothacker suggests that she be taken in by his mother and that she learn all the skills of managing an agricultural estate like his own. Katharina agrees, bids her father farewell, and leaves with Rothacker. Knie has misgivings, but he remains confident: "She will come back—she will come back!"[20]

This simple and uncluttered scenario is extended into Act Three. It is now a year later, and the troupe is performing again in the same market square. Despite Germany's intervening financial reforms, the Knie enterprise is not doing so well. Katharina returns briefly and, learning of the circumstances, she remarks: "But there is once more good money everywhere." To which a friend retorts: "But in the pocket of others."[21] Katharina explains that she has finished her early apprenticeship on the Rothacker estate, where she was always out in the fields, and she is now beginning a new phase in the gardens and vineyards. More significantly, she discloses that she intends soon to marry Martin Rothacker, and she promptly displays a ring to prove it. But the others should not tell her father; she wants to do that herself. When Father Knie joins them, he looks much older than before, yet he is determined—what else?—that the show must go on. And so it does when Knie musters all his remaining strength. Thereupon the emotional tangle of father, daughter, and her lover comes to a head. In her most touching moment Katharina tells Rothacker: "I have nothing else but you—and live only with you—and can no longer leave you! I cannot do otherwise. I have never before loved anyone so much—except my father [when] I knew only him. And now I know only you." Rothacker replies simply: "I'll think of you. I won't let you go."[22] But Katharina must confront her father that night. Before she gathers the courage to tell him the bittersweet truth, Knie delivers a soliloquy, which can be epitomized in a single sentence: "The main thing is that one knows where he belongs."[23] Then Katharina finally speaks: "I'm not staying here, father—I am leaving again—." Knie says nothing.[24]

Act Four is no more than an abbreviated postscript to tidy up the story and give it a kick at the end. Members of the Knie troupe are returning from a burial, manifestly sharing a feeling of emptiness. As Ignaz Scheel says: "A tightrope walker doesn't die every day." The audience must realize that he means Carl Knie. Julius the clown leaves no doubt: "Now the father lies in his grave."[25] Katharina is silent until she slips off her ring and offers it back to Rothacker while suddenly erupting: "I'm staying. I must stay!"[26] If not, she asks, what would come of the Knie troupe? She must take charge: "Are all the wagons ready? Then let's go! Hitch the horses! Avanti! Avanti!"[27]

Although Zuckmayer named his drama after the daughter Katharina, it is unquestionably Father Knie who dominates it. And when he dies, it ends. The qualities that had distinguished the two previous works, *Der fröhliche Weinberg* and *Schinderhannes*— which need not again be enumerated—also graced the conception of *Katharina Knie*. Regardless of what one may think of this arguably more minor dramatic effort, it gave further proof of Zuckmayer's remarkable ability to master another local dialect and carefully to observe the mannerisms and inflections necessary for actors to reproduce a realistic pageant on stage. Unfortunately, the charge by some critics against the play's slowness and sentimentality must stand. Action often proceeds at a glacial pace. And much of it occurs off-stage: the actual performances of the high wire troupe, Katharina's education and love affair at the Rothacker estate, and Father Knie's demise and death of a heart attack. It is Knie's growing weariness and loss of control that constitute the substance of Zuckmayer's script, and the sympathy of the audience must necessarily focus on his character. As for Katharina, she is of course central to the eternal triangle of father, daughter, and lover. Yet her behavior frequently seems skittish and flighty, hence largely inexplicable. At one instant she professes undying love for her fiancé, and in the next she abruptly throws him over and chooses to lead an uncertain vagabond existence with her father's troupe of tightrope artists. Zuckmayer thus invites his public to cheer her on, but he offers only vapid sentimental reasons to do so.

Chapter Seven

TWO GREAT HITS

It was a quantum leap for Carl Zuckmayer, in terms of public response as well as critical acclaim, from *Schinderhannes* and *Katharina Knie* to the play with which he entered the decade of the 1930s: *Der Hauptmann von Köpenick.* His astonishing success exceeded any previous triumph, even *Der fröhliche Weinberg,* and made him the most sought-after playwright in Central Europe. Above all, it consolidated Zuckmayer's reputation as Germany's leading author of comedic drama. Audiences roared with laughter at his inventive satire of the military and bureaucratic pomposities of prewar imperial Germany in a story, based on an actual incident, in which a down-and-out homeless cobbler impersonated an officer to commandeer the city hall of Köpenick (a southeastern suburb of Berlin). After 1945, even at the height of the Cold War, productions of *Der Hauptmann von Köpenick* were to be seen virtually everywhere in both West and East. The 1947 performance of it in Berlin was not especially to Zuckmayer's liking, though it was "significantly better than I had feared." Indeed, the play seemed almost "immortal" in Berlin, he observed. And it was meanwhile a "rousing success" in New York and "an absolutely sensational success" in London at the Old Vic. It was also staged in Paris, in East Berlin—for five consecutive years in the early 1960s—and in the eastern capital cities such as Warsaw, Bucharest, Budapest, etc., not to mention dozens of provincial theaters in Central Europe.[1]

Any summary or appraisal of Zuckmayer's script must face the sheer complexity of his conception, which was presented in twenty-one different scenes (seven in each of the three acts) and required a cast of seventy-three actors. It would therefore be tiresome to describe each and every scene from beginning to end, especially as the entire text to which they directly or indirectly contribute unfolds, despite this elaborate structure, with perfect clarity. The play's obvious central theme, a common German aphorism and the title of a short novel by Gottfried Keller, is more than once explicitly stated: *Kleider machen Leute* (clothes make the man).

Leading up to the hilarious concluding sequence, most of the action revolves around the miserable existence of a forlorn fifty-year old, Wilhelm Voigt, who has spent half of his life in confinement. His insoluble dilemma is easily defined as he describes it himself: Voigt cannot obtain a passport without employment, but he cannot find employment without a passport. Foiled again and again in his efforts to begin a decent life, he finally resorts to the desperate ruse indicated in Zuckmayer's title. He becomes the Captain von Köpenick. Until then Voigt likens his circumstance to that of a louse on a pane of glass, attempting to crawl up but repeatedly failing and instead slipping down. For some while he had worked at a shoe factory in eastern Europe, but he longed to regain his independence in the *Heimat* (homeland). As he puts it, in a moment recalling a similar lament by the father in *Katharina Knie,* "there must be a place where a man belongs."[2] Voigt encounters one Captain von Schlettow, who appears in mufti, feeling rather ill at ease. In uniform, he confides, a man cuts a more splendid figure: "one is a totally different fellow."[3] Later Schlettow is being fitted for a new uniform by his tailor, who remarks: "It's a work of art, Captain. That is not a jacket anymore. It is a better skin so to speak."[4] For his part, Voigt meanwhile attempts to break into police headquarters in Potsdam to remove his incriminating file. "Then I will begin again at the beginning."[5] But apprehended, he is sent to serve a sentence of ten years in the state penitentiary at Plötzensee near Berlin.

After his release, Voigt visits his respectable bourgeois family. His sister Marie is married to Friedrich Hoprecht, a proud member of the local militia reserve. With Voigt, his brother-in-law proves to be friendly and encouraging. "If I may predict," Friedrich says to him, "you will begin all over again. A man can always start anew. One is never too old for that."[6] In other scenes there is much more fussing about uniforms, moderately amusing situations in which Zuckmayer gently mocks the foibles of Germany's uncritical social esteem for all things military. Back with the Hoprechts, Voigt learns that Friedrich has failed to receive an expected promotion in the militia. "Total injustice," Voigt responds. Friedrich objects: it is necessary for a "healthy" society that everyone obeys and complies. Then where does injustice come from? Voigt asks. There is no injustice here, Friedrich counters. Conformity is required "for the fatherland and for the *Heimat!*" Voigt cannot bear to hear that nebulous German expression: "Where is then the *Heimat?* In a police office? Or here [pointing to his new eviction order from Prussia] in a paper?! I no longer see a *Heimat . . .!* "[7] Through such dialogue Voigt's exasperation and desperation are made manifest, thereby moving the scenario along toward a climax that every German theater fan was bound to anticipate.

Voigt's transformation occurs in a Potsdam costume shop, where an all too appropriate sign hangs conspicuously on the wall: *"Kleider machen Leute."* Voigt explains that he is slated to attend a masked ball and needs to rent a captain's uniform. After a few brusque incidents in his new attire, he boards a suburban train to Köpenick. Soon, from the foyer of the city hall there, Voigt's voice can be heard bellowing commands, ordering soldiers about, and demanding that the entrances be closed. With two armed soldiers, bayonets mounted, he then enters the office of Mayor Obermüller, where a portrait of Bismarck and a photo of the archconservative German philosopher

Arthur Schopenhauer are on display. Speaking now in *Hochdeutsch,* without a trace of Berlin dialect, Voigt arrests Obermüller in the name of the Kaiser and advises him that resistance is useless: "Orders are orders."[8] While he is at it, Voigt also withdraws over 4000 marks from the municipal treasury. All of this action transpires in two brief scenes, the eighteenth and nineteenth (of twenty-one). By the twentieth scene, Voigt is back in his civilian clothing, asleep on the bench of a pub in Berlin's downtown Friedrichstrasse. There a newspaper vendor arrives with a sensational extra, shouting *"Der Hauptmann von Köpenick."*[9]

In the play's final scene, Voigt is under arrest in the Berlin police headquarters. He affirms that he was indeed the now famous captain from Köpenick, but an attending police officer is skeptical of his claim. Can he prove it? Voigt admits that he cannot, but he asserts that his uniform is in a locked baggage compartment at a train station. The inspector remains unconvinced, assuming that Voigt's story is a bluff and that he is mentally unbalanced—until the uniform is brought in. Asked to put it on, Voigt does so, and he then requests a mirror so that he might for the first time see himself in full regalia. Standing with his back to the audience, he begins to shake and to laugh uncontrollably. He manages to utter only one word: "Impossible."[10]

A commentary is scarcely necessary. With this absorbing drama, Carl Zuckmayer's stagecraft reached its apex in the skillful use of a local dialect, the indelibly drawn characters, the fragmented yet totally comprehensible plot development, and the rich satirical thrust of the vivid settings and dialogue. Zuckmayer's genius—a word that does not seem unfitting here—swept the German stage with infectious gusto. Needless to add, however, not everyone was amused. The public delight was hardly shared by the political far right, and particularly by the leadership of the rising Nazi Party. Zuckmayer's satirical edge cut deeply to the quick of Joseph Goebbels and his cohort. No wonder, then, that less than two years after its premier in March 1931, *Der Hauptmann von Köpenick* was banned from all German theaters and its author was hounded into exile.

Carl Zuckmayer's long residence in America during the Second World War took him away from everything he had hitherto known in his life and career. Accordingly, there was an extended pause in his literary production. Yet this break proved beneficial insofar as it afforded him the opportunity to ponder some ideas that he began in early 1943 to formulate in a dramatic script. What emerged by war's end was Zuckmayer's most serious narrative, *Des Teufels General* (*The Devil's General*), which was to remain one of the most frequently performed stage plays in Europe during the ensuing twenty years. It premiered in Zürich near the end of 1946 and was first presented in Germany at Frankfurt in 1947.

The story concerns General Harras—familiarly called "Harry" by his friends—a prominent officer in the German Luftwaffe who is directly responsible for the production and procurement of military aircraft. Harras is an imposing figure, commanding in his manner but genial and generous in his private contacts with others. It is not at all far-fetched to regard Harras as an idealized version of Zuckmayer himself, the sort of person he might wish to be were he not banned and exiled from his homeland. The similarity between author and fictional hero was not simply external but also reflected the psychological essence of their problematic existence. The question was: how was one to reconcile devotion to the German nation with contempt for it current Nazi leadership. For Zuckmayer the only recourse was exile; yet in his imagination, Harras had other possibilities.

The play recounts a complex set of circumstances leading to its tragic conclusion. The setting is Berlin late in 1941, shortly before America's entry into the great conflict that had already enveloped Europe. The staging of Act One occurs in a fancy restaurant at a buffet party hosted by Harras for some of his more intimate acquaintances. He enters—"bright, open, charming, and a bit cunning"—while just arriving from a Bierabend of the Führer.[11] About age 45, he is still dashing and youthful, a magnet for the ladies of high society. Despite the presence of a Nazi representative (clearly intended to resemble Joseph Goebbels) from the Ministry of Propaganda (or *"Propapopogandamysterium,"* as Harras likes to call it), he is at ease in ridiculing the party's bigwigs: "When in Berlin there is talk about the father, it is always about fat Hermann [Göring], our Reichsmarshal with a spare tire around the middle."[12]

Women enter, among them another officer's wife, the elegant Anne Eilers, and her "rather shrill" sister. During the ensuing flirtatious conversation, almost incidentally, Harras mentions a report about technically defective airplanes. He is overheard by the propaganda man, Dr. Schmidt-Lausitz, and the two match wits. Schmidt-Lausitz professes to know nothing about technology: "My specialty is culture. Total mobilization of the German spirit. You know. And enlightenment of neutral countries. That is also battle, albeit not with weapons."[13] Harras denies both technological and ideological skill: "I have never been a Nazi. I am a pilot, nothing more."[14] As he is responsible for the entire Luftwaffe, however, he must deal with the suspicions of sabotage, "reported with a certain regularity." To do so, he will rely on his engineer, Oderbruch, who cannot fail to uncover the truth.[15]

This banter is lightened by the entrance of Olivia Geiss (an old flame of Harras) and her gorgeous niece, Diddo. In a private moment apart with Harras, Olivia confides that her niece is already completely smitten with him. Thus a subplot is established that shows the softer side of Harras without unduly distracting from the development of far more sinister matters, which are underscored in one of the play's longest and most intense scenes, an exchange between Harras and an idealistic young air force officer named Hartmann. Mistakenly assuming their views on the glory of military heroism are identical, Hartmann speaks aloud: "Yes indeed, Herr General. Death on the battlefield is great and pure and eternal." Harras cuts him short: "Ah shit . . . Death on the battlefield stinks, I'll tell you. It is vulgar and raw and filthy." Nowhere does the actor speak more pointedly for the author.[16]

In his memoirs, we recall, Zuckmayer relates how he wrote the opening act of *Des Teufels General* within three weeks in one sudden burst of creative enthusiasm but then labored over the rest of his drama for the next two years.[17] It is not difficult to understand why. The ambiance of Act One is a festive evening party, Zuckmayer's favorite milieu, where the various characters can easily come and go as the dialogue rolls on. Despite the foreboding news of sabotage and the menacing presence of Schmidt-Lausitz, the tone remains almost lilting until the concluding clash between Harras and Hartmann. In the succeeding two acts, to the contrary, the situation becomes darker and more troubled, lending it an atmosphere in which Zuckmayer, a master of comedy, was far less practiced. If the remainder of the drama is more tightly constructed, therefore, it lacks the same spontaneity and flow of the initial sequences and instead plunges the audience into a hushed concentration on the mounting emotional turmoil taking place on stage.

The pace of Act Two is somewhat meandering at times, yet it brings Harras convincingly to a point of crisis. It is unclear, let it be said, what purpose of Zuckmayer is served by introducing an American journalist, Buddy Lawrence, except to provide some idle chatter in English. Probably Zuckmayer intended thereby to show off his command of an adopted language; but, if so, a few minor grammatical errors rather undercut that attempt.[18] Much more entertaining are the sweet nothings between Harras and his young lover Diddo. He greets her tenderly: "You have changed. You have become older. More beautiful." They exchange kisses and playfully flaunt their mutual admiration.[19]

Altogether different is a brief sequence with Diddo's aunt, Olivia Geiss. Dr. Samuel Bergmann, a Jewish friend who had already endured six months in the concentration camp of Buchenwald, has committed suicide with his wife. Upon hearing that news, Olivia faints and is laid out on a couch, whereas Harras is wild with rage: "Everyone has a Jew on his conscience, or many. Thus we are guilty for what happens to thousands of others we do not know and do not help. Guilty and damned for all eternity. Permitting evil is worse than doing it." Obviously, for Harras it is a decisive moment of self-accusation.[20]

This outburst is succeeded by Diddo's departure from Harras, resulting from the report of another fatality: Anne Eilers's husband, also a Luftwaffe pilot, who has just died in an accident due to a defective plane. The Führer has ordered a state funeral for him. Harras knows that he has been given ten days to investigate possible sabotage, and the consequences of failing to resolve the issue are likely to be grave for him. He must therefore be certain that Diddo meanwhile reaches safety, and he urges her to flee to Vienna. Reluctantly, though knowing full well that his advice is likely to separate them for good, she bows to his wishes and agrees to depart. With that, plot and sub-plot are merged, both irrepressibly heading toward an unhappy end.[21]

Finally, for the first time Oderbruch is thrust into the action. He is a slender man, slightly younger than Harras but without the General's personal allure. Oderbruch was a close friend of the deceased Eilers, yet he seems unshaken. He is pressed by Harras for an explanation of this latest accident: "Do you know something?" Oderbruch replies enigmatically: "Only the facts."[22]

As one must expect, the truth is soon revealed in the much briefer Act Three, set at the office of a military air base in Berlin. There can no longer be the slightest doubt that they are dealing with deliberate sabotage. And Harras, although innocent of any crime, must bear the responsibility. He is confronted with that painful reality in a devastating confrontation with the now widowed Anne Eilers, an exchange that forms the crux of the play and deserves quotation:

Harras: "What are you accusing me of, Anne? What have I done?"

Anne: "You have done nothing. One does not act without belief. You did not believe what Eilers did. And yet, you allowed him to die. Senseless death. You watched and did not save him. That is a guilt for which there is no pardon . . . You could have saved him . . . You are a murderer. Eilers was a hero."

Disarmed, Harras fumbles for an excuse. Then he releases his anguish with a cry: "Who am I then? Am I more than a man? Can I know more —do more—suffer more than a man? I am not—I am not a God."[23]

At last Harras cannot avoid directing his suspicions to his most trusted underling Oderbruch and demands from him the truth. Haltingly Oderbruch offers it: "The enemy is elusive. He stands everywhere . . . In the midst of our people . . . In the midst of our ranks. And if he wins, Harras . . . If Hitler wins this war . . . Then Germany is lost. Then the world is lost."[24] To this statement Harras finds no adequate response. Instead, he abruptly picks up the telephone and calls the propaganda emissary Schmidt-Lausitz to announce that within minutes the case will be closed. Oderbruch suggests that his superior find a refuge in Switzerland, but Harras waves him off: whoever has become the devil's general must make his nest in hell. He leaves and climbs into an airplane. The audience hears only the roar of an engine, but the outcome is evident to everyone. It is left to the despicable Dr. Schmidt-Lausitz to announce it in a telephone call to his headquarters: "General Harras has just died in an accident while fulfilling his duty. While testing a fighter plane. Yes. State funeral."[25]

Only through quotation can the compelling intensity of *Des Teufels General* be aptly conveyed. A bland summary, no matter how perceptive, would not do. "State funeral" for example. Alone, those two words express like nothing else possibly could the irony of the main character's death as well as the thinly disguised cynicism of his Nazi nemesis. Despite the humiliating confession of complicity

104

with their fascist regime by the German people after 1933—in terms not of collective guilt but of individual responsibility—Carl Zuckmayer's vision won enthusiastic public praise but not universal critical approval. Although the play that he brought from Vermont was certainly seen as a serious drama, there was sometimes a charge that the principal characters too often verged on caricature placed on the stage by the author merely to express certain programmatic ideas. Thus the effect was to depart from the realistic dialogue of his earlier scripts and to adopt a stilted and rather preachy tone. Sensitive to this negative professional reaction, Zuckmayer later recast portions of his text, managing only to raise additional doubts about what should be regarded as the definitive version?[26] That said, *Des Teufels General* nonetheless joined *Der fröhliche Weinberg* and *Der Hauptmann von Köpenick* among Carl Zuckmayer's most notable literary achievements, a reputation enhanced by several film productions of his work that enjoyed a worldwide popularity in the immediate postwar years.

Chapter Eight

AFTER THE WAR

In some regards *Des Teufels General* must be seen as an anomaly. Gone were the typical traits of Zuckmayer's earlier works during the Weimar Republic: the local patois, the heavy doses of folklore, the rowdy antics of a setting in pubs and speakeasies. The quiet contemplation of Vermont nights, far from the homeland he knew and often portrayed, had visibly moved him to conceive a narrative and adopt a speech quite different from the stage productions that had previously contributed to his lofty station as a German playwright. Precisely those qualities seemed altogether inappropriate after the fall of the Third Reich. But in the postwar years Zuckmayer reverted to form, only to learn that Germany was then a place with little taste for his formerly practiced joviality. After 1945 he managed to finish a half dozen new plays, but to little avail. Briefly two of them are worthy of mention here.

Der Gesang im Feuerofen was in many ways a curious choice of subjects for Zuckmayer. Presumably he hoped to repeat the generally positive reception of *Des Teufels General* by relating an episode that took place in Lyon in 1948 when a Frenchman was tried and convicted of collaborating with the Gestapo during the wartime German occupation of France. Reports of the trial led Zuckmayer to an extended and elaborate reflection on the Franco-German relationship and in particular on the role of the French resistance movement. Once more the strain between long-standing patriotism to the nation and military action against its current government (the Vichy regime) was evident. While Zuckmayer could gather details of the court case and the surrounding wartime circumstances from newspaper articles, he found no way to imitate in German the speech pattern of ordinary French citizens who comprised the bulk of maquis recruits. He seemed uncertain, moreover, of whether to confine himself to a rendition of historical facts or to indulge in theatrical fantasy. Thus the trajectory of the play was repeatedly disturbed by mythical scenes featuring the paper maché figures of Mother Frost, Father Wind, Brother Fog, and a host of fluttering angels. Their function was to comment on the action much like a Greek chorus of ancient times, a contrivance that earned the approbation neither of the public nor the critics.

Yet Zuckmayer had high hopes for his drama. In early 1950, writing in English to an American acquaintance, he announced that it would soon be ready, "and I seriously believe it will be the best and perhaps the most important play I've written."[1] To his consternation, not for the first time, the theater world evinced little enthusiasm for his effort. Hence, a decade later, he could not repress his disappointment. "I am attached to this play. It is a 'love child' of mine that I find unjustly criticized and neglected." Consequently, during the 1960s he continued to lament that his masterpiece failed to receive the adulation it deserved. "I still consider this play to be one of my best and most important." And again, reacting to a compliment about it, he persisted: "For me, too, *Der Gesang im Feuerofen* is the most precious of my dramatic works."[2] Why, then, such indifference? Zuckmayer himself offered a caustic but correct diagnosis. Whereas the play had enjoyed a great success at Vienna's Burgtheater when it first appeared, by 1970 it was no longer considered to be timely. "What is timely," he remarked, "is now decided by the anti-dramatists." Occasional praise from a few individual fans did not mitigate his regret that his accomplishment had become "curiously too little known."[3] Such comments are surely evidence enough of Zuckrnayer's waning popularity in the postwar years once the initial wave of excitement about *Der Hauptmann von Köpenick* and *Des Teufels General* had passed.

Suffering from some of the same problems, apart from its awkward title, was one of Zuckmayer's final efforts, *Das Leben des Horace A. W. Tabor,* first performed in Zürich in 1964. Apparently he had first heard of this sob story while living in the United States. The setting is the scruffy mining town of Leadville, Colorado, deep in the

Rocky Mountains. There a wealthy silver mine owner falls desperately in love with a young woman, divorces his wife, and then marries "Baby Doe." Their relationship is passionate but of short duration due to Tabor's death, leaving the miserable heroine to pine away for nearly forty years in a shabby little wooden hut (still a tourist attraction) at the Matchless Mine. Again, as when dealing with a scenario set in France, Zuckmayer faced the insoluble task of inventing appropriate dialogue for foreign characters with whom he was not closely familiar. The contrived drama centered on the rise and fall of an American silver king thus made little impression in a divided Germany locked in the Cold War.

It is worth noting that, unknown to Zuckmayer, a brilliantly melodic opera by the American composer Douglas Moore, entitled *The Ballad of Baby Doe,* had at the same time appeared on the American stage. To gather information for his play Zuckmayer had relied on nothing more than a long article in the *Saturday Evening Post* and some non-fictional accounts of Colorado mining. During the final stage of preparation, barely six months before the premier, he asked his friend and future biographer Arnold John Jacobius for additional historical material. In reply, Jacobius informed him of Moore's production, which henceforth Zuckmayer (without seeing it) rather slightingly referred to as a *"Volksoper"* or, with an even more belittling phrase, as "a kind of musical."[4] Yet his own piece suffered the same fate as *Der Gesang im Feuerofen.* After its premier in Zürich

109

Tabor failed to become a staple of European or American theater, much to Zuckmayer's disgust. To another correspondent he wrote in December 1965: "I am especially attached to this play," in spite of the verdict of critics who think it "unmodern." He continued: it has been "fundamentally misunderstood and quite dismissively treated by many critical dolts *(Eselköpfe)*." Yet, a few months later, when sounded out by the Bavarian radio network about the possibility of presenting his latest work in a broadcast, Zuckmayer declined, while conceding that the rejection of it by his critics "was not entirely wrong." This begrudging self-contradiction offers some hint of the dismay and confusion that marked the final decade of his life.[5]

By placing Carl Zuckmayer's more arresting theatrical accomplishments end to end, stretching over a period of more than half a century, it is only fair to conclude that he was one of Germany's most prolific and distinguished playwrights in the twentieth century and, at least during the Weimar years, also among the most popular. But that leaves open the question of how we should evaluate his talent and how we should rank him among German authors who wrote primarily for the stage at that time. Three observations in that regard appear to be valid.

First of all, it is apparent that Zuckmayer should not be counted among those to whom the all too elastic label of "Expressionism" has been attached. They were in fact a heterogeneous group of playwrights, including such diverse figures as Ernst Toller, Georg Kaiser, Georg Heim, Franz Werfel, and Fritz von Unruh. They had ruled the German stage during the final decades of Imperial Germany before the First World War, but they slowly lost their grip thereafter. In general their works depended heavily on symbolism, and they did not feel themselves bound to restrict themselves to a realistic setting. The only one of Zuckmayer's works that could possibly be so classified was the earliest, *Kreuzweg,* written in 1920; and it proved to be a critical and commercial disaster. The characters were unhistorical, drawn from legend, and their declamations were hardly those of everyday life either past or present. Clearly, to be successful, the young author would need a change of course.

Second, in the years following, Zuckmayer made such a change by adopting a much more realistic style. He thereby played to his strength: namely, an ability carefully to mimic the speech patterns of individuals, to focus on and to develop specific human events, and to portray the actions and reactions of crowds that often flooded the stage in his plays. These talents were fused again and again in scripts written in regional dialects, a skill for which he had no major rival and which extended from the ever popular *Der fröhliche Weinberg* through his universally revered *Der Hauptmann von Köpenick.* True, his last important drama, *Des Teufels General,* was written largely in *Hochdeutsch,* the common tongue of educated people in all of Central Europe; but that, too, was an appropriate linguistic rendition of speech among military officers in the German Luftwaffe. All of these plays had an identifiable historical location, a tightly constructed dramatic setting, and an emphasis on the human element of characters, who needed no symbolic gestures or soaring monologues to advance their individuality. In short, Zuckmayer found just the right formula to suit his time and place.

Third, precisely those traits did not serve Zuckmayer well after 1945 when Germany was recovering from the shock of war and repairing the ruins of defeat. Zuckmayer's longstanding sense of humor and bonhomie could only feel inappropriate for a nation recuperating from a disaster with shame and humiliation. The problem for Zuckmayer was not merely a matter of technique. By nature he was a genial and jovial man for whom the intimacy of many personal relationships came easily. Even the tragic circumstances presented in *Des Teufels General* did not preclude a sympathetic (not to say sentimental) portrait of General Harras or his flirtatious advances with young women. Yet the imputation was inescapable that Zuckmayer was too often guilty in the postwar era of purveying trivialities and failing to adapt to new circumstances the style that had formed and nourished his career before 1933.

An additional comment is in place here. One of the distinctive traits of Zuckmayer as a playwright was his talent for creating vital leading roles for male actors. One has only to look down the list of central characters in his pantheon of drama. To name only the most obvious: Christian Kutter, Jean Baptiste Gunderloch, Johann Bückler, Father Knie, Wilhelm Voigt, Horace Tabor. In every sense of the term, they tended to be large men with imposing physiques and staunch personalities—even Wilhelm Voigt once he was fitted with his officer's uniform. Zuckmayer's plays were above all about them, whether they enjoyed grand success or suffered dismal failure. Any analysis of his corpus of work could not avoid noting, and it bears repeating, that a ubiquitous scent of autobiography permeated Zuckmayer's texts, as if he were reliving his own emotions and desires through a presentation about the fate of one protagonist after another. Critics have generally therefore given Zuckmayer due credit for his portrayal of dominant males.

But perhaps he deserves no less praise for his skillful rendering of female roles.[6] Again the list is long and impressive: Christa, Klärchen, Annemarie, Julchen, Katharina, Diddo, Baby Doe. Usually cast as the daughter or lover of the hero, these women were invariably younger, more vulnerable, and irresistibly endearing—exactly the sort of partners, one must observe, that Zuckmayer himself had often courted.

All things considered, then, it is possible to locate chronologically the strict limit of Carl Zuckmayer's contribution to the evolving world of German theater. He belonged neither to the playwrights of pre-1918 nor to those of post-1945. Indeed, except for the marvelous exception of *Des Teufels General*, written in exile and isolation, his career was effectively cut short by the advent of the Nazi regime, thereby further narrowing the scope of his best work to fifteen years. At the least it can be said that during that decade and a half Zuckmayer's plays were performed more frequently than those of any other dramatist in Central Europe. That singular achievement is surely sufficient to place Zuckmayer among the most significant stage authors of the early twentieth century.

Chapter Nine

IN HEALTH AND SICKNESS

In the age of Twitter and Facebook one can only marvel at the lost art of letter writing as it was still practiced in the early twentieth century. Habits had begun to change after the invention of the typewriter in the late nineteenth century. But it was not uncommon that a single epistle would cover eight or ten or twelve pages—sometimes hand-written, sometimes typed—a document that might take hours to compose even for a fluent author like Carl Zuckmayer. Large collections of his personal correspondence have been published and are accessible in university libraries; but there is no substitute for the voluminous cartons of originals that are to be found in abundance at the Deutsches Literaturarchiv at Marbach-am-Neckar and that constitute the principal basis of this chapter and the next.

Much is to be learned about Zuckmayer from these spontaneous compositions, which revealed personal and professional details that are well beyond formal treatments of his life or indeed the account of his own autobiographical recollections that was drafted many years after the events described. Here it is well to scan these letters in order to discover at firsthand how Zuckmayer experienced his most productive years as a playwright during the troubled time of the Weimar Republic that culminated in the eruption of Nazism in Germany, and also how he fared in later years. Rather than to follow a neat chronological pattern, it seems best in this instance to single out various themes that recurred in his letters concerning the era in question.

It is no surprise that much of Zuckmayer's attention in his correspondence of the 1920s was devoted to theater, to politics in general, and of course to his own failures and successes as a playwright, which have already been amply documented. The record from the opening of that decade is sparse, and one may surmise that his early blunders were a painful topic that he preferred only rarely and briefly to discuss. Yet in January 1923 Zuckmayer did unburden himself in a letter to his friend Albrecht Joseph with a long confession (of eight hand-written pages) about his unhappiness at the theater in Kiel, where there was "agitation" to dismiss him after a flood of unfavorable reviews of his fledgling stage productions. To this admission, he could only add: "I regret my mistakes."[1] It was with some relief, then, that he found his way back to Berlin where "it smells like theater." For instance, one thing he noticed at the

Deutsches Theater on the Gendarmenmarkt was that all the actors, even those cast in minor roles, played their part with unrestrained enthusiasm.[2]

Finally, at the end of December 1925 Zuckmayer had his first hit, and the tone of his letters suddenly reflected it. Writing to his mother-in-law, he could boast about the soon forthcoming premiers of *Der fröhliche Weinberg* in Berlin, Frankfurt, Munich, Hamburg, Mannheim, and Leipzig. He had been awarded the Kleist Prize and signed to a contract with the Ullstein publishing house that rescued his miserable finances for the immediate future.[3] None of Zuckmayer's other plays aroused such pride until the appearance of *Der Hauptmann von Köpenick* in March 1931. Several weeks before the Berlin premier he had typed eight pages again to Albrecht Joseph in which he recounted the last minute preparations for the opening. All at once there were so many premiers that he could not attend every one. But he did not fail to confide his delight at the "fantastic success" in Essen, the "enormous success" in Vienna, and so on.[4] Zuckmayer's public pose was one of unfailing modesty. But his correspondence thus showed a justifiable gratification that he had become a genuine luminary of German theater. We know, however, that his enjoyment of such prestige was brief, since the Nazis had a rather different opinion of his work.

It is noteworthy that Zuckmayer was usually an extremely poor judge of his own literary efforts. In an article published in 1928 he briefly reviewed the series of his failures earlier in that decade. He confessed that he was altogether astonished by the popular and critical acclaim reaped by *Der fröhliche Weinberg,* "which I myself considered a bagatelle." He thought the play's prospects for success would be confined to the small area where his Rhenish dialect was spoken, and therefore its widespread acceptance came as such a surprise "that I almost fainted."[5] He was meanwhile working on the adaptation of an American play, *What Price Glory* by Maxwell Anderson and Laurence Stallings, which appeared in Europe entitled *Rivalen.* It was, he imagined, "especially successful" and thus "one of my most accomplished works." This self-tribute was scarcely shared in Central Europe, as the drama was greeted there with yawning indifference.[6]

Zuckmayer was particularly annoyed that his reputation was based solely on his stage scenarios, whereas his novellas and poetry remained virtually unknown. That circumstance might be bettered, he thought, when he published his first novel, which he believed to have every chance to find worldwide interest—as it proved, another erroneous judgment.[7] To his credit, however, Zuckmayer was warming to a recognition that the métier of a novelist was not his true calling: "Certainly my deepest passion, as always, belongs to the theater."[8] He might better have written: to the theater in Europe. Once the Nazis came to power, we know, his passion had to wait. During his exile in the United States, he hoped by a masterful fusion of translation and adaptation to make a leap onto the American stage. It never occurred.[9]

Almost a full decade later, near the end of the 1940s, after *Der Hauptmann von Köpenick* and *Des Teufels General* had firmly established Zuckmayer among the elite of European theater, he continued to strive for confirmation of his enhanced standing. His expectations were especially high for a new play called *Barbara Blomberg,* which premiered in the spring of 1949. While putting the finishing touches on this work just before its opening, he referred to it in a private letter as "my strongest and also most beautiful play." But the public did not agree, alas, and Zuckmayer was forced to endure another flop. In fact, as noted previously, none of his postwar productions lived up to his high expectations.[10] Even the last of his dramatic compositions, *Kranichtanz (Dance of the Cranes),* a complex one-act play that premiered in Zürich in 1967, by no means fulfilled Zuckmayer's ambitions for it. As late as April 1976, less than a year before his death, he continued to eulogize his own literary efforts. Despite some withering criticism, while writing from Saas-Fee to the director of a recent production of *Kranichtanz* in Göttingen, he insisted: "I myself consider it my best play—which in view of *Der Hauptmann von Köpenick* may perhaps sound ridiculous—but I believe (like you) that I have created here a true tragedy."[11] Better also than *Des Teufels General,* or than a half dozen of his other earlier works? Scarcely a single critic, past or present, could agree.

Zuckmayer's correspondence reveals that he suffered throughout his career from frequent disruptions due to a variety of often severe afflictions that plagued him to the end. Attempting to piece together his personal health record from references in scores of letters is understandably to confront a complex puzzle. Yet one thing is certain: he endured far more physical disability in his adult life than one might suspect from his other autobiographical writings. Such problems began early, at the age of ten, when he broke his leg while at play. His comment on that event in 1930, when writing to Annemarie Suhrkamp ("Mirl"), was concise: "The right leg had to be somewhat shortened [and] a slight limp remained."[12] This handicap must have been minor, given Zuckmayer's military service in the First World War, but the injuries inflicted on him during those four years— among them shrapnel wounds and a "brain concussion"— took time to heal.[13] Other difficulties followed. In the summer of 1922 Zuckmayer developed stomach trouble that threatened an ulcer. Forbidden to drink his beloved Schnaps, he was limited to white wine (hardly a severe restriction in the Rhineland).[14] Upset in the first years of marriage also led to an unidentified malady that, when it finally lifted in 1928, gave him the feeling of recovering from a sapping fever. Again in 1931 he became "seriously ill," a bout of bad health, "unpleasant and exhausting," which prevented him from traveling for a time. During those "awful days" caused by an inflammation of the throat, he completely lost his voice for a short time and was required to visit a medical specialist every morning and evening to receive injections. The entire episode was "uncommonly dangerous," he concluded, but not lasting.[15]

Remarkably, Zuckmayer's ailments seemed to abate during the long stretch of exile in Austria and America during the Nazi period. From Vermont he wrote in 1942 that the winters there were hard, but "thank God our health has always been good."[16]

Before leaving after the war for the return to Europe, soon after finishing *Des Teufels General,* he could boast that he was now "productive as never before in my life."[17] But by the autumn of 1948 he was stricken by a "rather severe" heart condition. An electrocardiogram proved to be "somewhat disturbing," and he began to realize that he was experiencing the onset of a coronary thrombosis that was not "directly dangerous now but must be taken very seriously." Cruelly for a bon vivant like Zuckmayer, as punishment he was forced to give up cigars and Schnaps, whereupon he was committed for several months to a sanatorium: "for the first time in my life I was seriously ill." If that statement did not quite accord with his earlier health record, it was accurate that at age fifty-three he was in effect laid low by a heart attack.[18] He remained in medical confinement until early 1950 after his physician informed him that it would take a full year for his recovery. "But I didn't want to believe it," he quipped, "until I was lying flat on my face."[19]

For Zuckmayer, the 1950s were marginally better. Starting in the autumn of 1956, however, he had to deal with an "eccentric infection" accompanied by high fever that left him unable to work for weeks at a time. By the end of the decade it turned out that he had contracted a virus that led to a bad cold, bronchitis, and possibly pneumonia. Once more he ended in a hospital and then a sanatorium for treatment and rest.[20] By now, nearing the age of seventy, Zuckmayer attempted to resume what for him was a normal pace—attending performances of his plays in Germany, flying to New York, visiting the old farm in Vermont—but it was "a bit too much," and he suffered a "collapse" of his circulatory system. He returned to Europe by ship, sleeping twelve hours a day, and felt once again fit, only to endure a "difficult but successful kidney operation" in May 1965. This was compounded by another viral infection that left him "rather seriously ill" and indeed, as he said, in danger for his life during "almost a month." No wonder he was still feeling "rather miserable" by the spring of 1966.[21]

The year following brought no improvement. "My health at the moment is not the best," he confessed, and it became dramatically worse during a vacation in Italy in early 1967 when he tripped and fell. Once more he sustained a concussion. At first, his condition did not seem serious this time, with few obvious ill effects beyond a slight headache for which a local physician merely prescribed some pills. Yet, after his return to Switzerland, Zuckmayer had "a total collapse." He "simply fell and was gone." Rushed to the hospital in an ambulance, he did not as feared require a brain operation, but x-rays showed a small split in his skull. As if that were not enough, he had to undergo a second sinus operation that autumn, and he continued to suffer "nasty back pains" due to ligament damage from his most recent accident.[22]

Admittedly, lying flat on one's face is not an ideal posture for creative writing. Which is to say that the noticeable decline in Carl Zuckmayer's literary prowess and productivity during his final decade must have had physical as well as intellectual explanations. The list of his various ailments after the mid-1960s was long and disheartening. To pursue them all further would serve little purpose, although the documentation of them is conspicuously abundant in his correspondence. They included urological complications, another bad fall requiring stitches, another sinus infection, a cataract operation, a kidney infection, a lung infection, another heart attack, bronchitis again, and finally an intractable weakening of the heart that lingered throughout 1976 and led to Zuckmayer's death in the year following.[23] He met these infirmities and indignities with extraordinary resilience, as one can observe in the many photos of this charming and thoughtful senior passing the dwindling days of his life in Saas-Fee. In sum, although the scattered references in his letters hardly disclose a complete medical analysis, they display a much bleaker aspect of Zuckmayer's physical condition than the happy-go-lucky image that he generally sought to project in public, and they deserve to be reported in any comprehensive account of his biography.

Chapter Ten

FRIENDS AND LOVERS

It is manifestly impossible within a limited space to map out the entirety of Carl Zuckmayer's intimate personal relationships. Yet it is surely worthwhile to probe into his correspondence, which stretched over half of the twentieth century from the 1920s to the 1970s and which thereby yields an invaluable trove of information and opinion drawn from his experience. During that time Zuckmayer wrote literally thousands of letters: some of them of course scattered or discarded, though many others have been preserved for posterity. They are naturally not simple to classify, extending as they do from brief and often trivial messages to lengthy disquisitions. Their recipients, as one would expect, ranged from various individuals obscure and now forgotten to the famous historical personalities who figure in any standard account of modern Germany.

By no means was Zuckmayer one whose close friends were invariably among the most notable of his era. In this regard, two categories come immediately to mind: schoolboy or student comrades, and the numerous acquaintances from his career in theater and film. Included among the former were never prominent names like the local Mainz chums Carlo Mierendorff and Theodor Heubach, the minor poet Hans Schiebelhuth, a Swiss reporter for the *Neue Zürcher Zeitung* Josef Halperin, the gentlemanly publisher Henry Goverts, and the Hungarian novelist Ödön von Horváth. All of them played an occasional role throughout Zuckmayer's autobiography, one of the rare books today in which their names are to be found. And as for Zuckmayer's professional life, it is striking that he most often chose to carouse with actors whose identity was seldom if ever illuminated by the bright theater lights, which are in any case now extinguished. A few did achieve some notoriety—Gustaf Gründgens, Emil Jannings, and Werner Krauss for example—but their reputations have also largely faded. Zuckmayer likewise socialized with a number of illustrious stage and film directors of that era like Erich Engel, Heinz Hilpert, Hans Kupper, Alexander Korda, Ernst Lubitsch, and the still remembered Berlin impresario Max Reinhardt. This listing is incomplete but adequate to suggest the breadth and depth of Zuckmayer's peer group.

One name stands out on the roster of today's nearly anonymous personalities: Albrecht Joseph. Before 1945 he and Zuckmayer were the closest of attentive friends, exchanging dozens of letters enough to fill a collected volume of 460 pages.[1] They first met in a restroom in Kiel, at a time when Zuckmayer was smarting from the abrupt end to his affair with Annemarie Seidel; and he did so, Joseph reliably observed, by conducting as many love trysts as possible with other women. He was nonetheless open, lively, and ever charming with his male friends, and he always displayed "a high degree of intelligence."[2] Over the years, the two discussed all manner of persons and events in the most confidential terms—until Joseph read the manuscript of Zuckmayer's *Des Teufels General,* at which he took irreconcilable offense. "His political thought is repulsive," Joseph wrote, and for good measure he explained: "I will always refuse to approve of the positive [and] creative aspect that Zuckmayer finds in war and violence."[3] Whether that harsh judgment was appropriate is debatable, but it led to a complete breakup. They last spoke with one another in New York City in 1945, and a frigid tone settled thereafter into their correspondence. Whereas Zuckmayer then returned to Europe, Joseph remained as an inconspicuous functionary in the American film industry until his death in 1972.

With his distinction as a German playwright already established in the 1920s, Zuckmayer could scarcely avoid contacts with the greats and near-greats of his generation. Two of them qualified for him among the "seniors of German literature": Gerhart Hauptmann and Thomas Mann.[4] More than thirty years older than Zuckmayer, Hauptmann (who had a residence near Henndorf in Austria) exchanged courteous and respectful pleasantries with him, but nothing beyond that. Somewhat less ancient, Thomas Mann was one of those with whom Zuckmayer often conversed in Salzburg during the 1930s. Mann had first written to him in 1931 after attending a stage production of *Der Hauptmann von Köpenick*, which he generously praised as "the best comedy in world literature" since Gogol.[5] Yet in the year following he sent a stiff formal note to "Lieber Herr Zuckmayer," signing it as "Ihr Ergebener Thomas Mann," just as impersonal as could be. For his part, Zuckmayer initially admired Mann's outspoken condemnation of Nazism but then vigorously objected to the notion of the "collective guilt" of the German people as advocated by Mann and his daughter Erika.[6]

Zuckmayer's correspondence bears out the generalization that, in spite of his early leanings toward the socialist left, he remained essentially unpolitical in any party sense of the term. Regarding three veterans from the bizarre eruption of the Bavarian Soviet Republic in 1919, he knew Gustav Landauer only slightly, Erich Mühsam rather well (albeit at a distance), and Ernst Toller best of all. After his release from prison, Toller came to Berlin and cultivated there a close relationship with Zuckmayer *(per Du)*. Zuckmayer later had to admit, however, that Toller remained "always entirely alien."[7]

Zuckmayer also pursued friendships with younger engaged German leftists such as Tankred Dorst and Günter Grass, both political activists as well as outstanding literary figures during the Cold War. He attempted to excuse himself to Grass for not joining ranks with them by explaining that nonetheless he was, "now as always, for Social Democracy." And he expressed his admiration for the personal engagement by Grass in the public arena: "You know exactly what you are doing and are completely informed about the political landscape of the present *Bundesrepublik*—which is not the case with me."[8] Understandably, as his health worsened in the 1970s, he was even less inclined to public agitation for the socialist cause, however worthy it was.

There were others who ought at least to be mentioned. Although Zuckmayer formally remained a Roman Catholic, as an adult he showed as little partisanship in religious as in political matters. One evidence of that virtual neutrality was his lengthy exchanges with the famous Protestant theologian Karl Barth, who late in life became a professor at the University of Basel. Regularly addressing letters to Barth as "dear friend" and "dear honored friend," Zuckmayer came as close as ever to articulating his abiding faith: "I belong to those for whom God is *not* dead" and who believe that Christianity, "when properly grasped and experienced, [is] still the gospel."[9] Barth, in return, paid a cordial visit to the Zuckmayers in Saas-Fee. The same was true of Theodor Heuss, then President of the Bonn Republic, with whom Zuckmayer exchanged a host of letters—also beginning with "dear honored friend"—and who likewise took the time to pay the Zuckmayers a visit.[10] Finally, this group would not be complete without reference to Oskar Kokoschka, whom Zuckmayer had known since his student days in Heidelberg, where "OK" was "our God." A half century later Kokoschka was still a master of the arts, "among the many splendid painters of his time the greatest," in Zuckmayer's opinion. Writing to Kokoschka on the eve of his eightieth birthday in 1967, Zuckmayer confidently assured him that he would live forever.[11]

Of all Zuckmayer's most notable friends the closest to him was probably Stefan Zweig, to whom he devoted six pages of uninterrupted accolades in his autobiography. To be sure, in some respects Zweig was "a strange bird." But once he had befriended someone like Zuckmayer, he offered "limitless, loving brotherhood" expressed with "perhaps unique generosity and helpfulness." An example, in Zuckmayer's case, was the gift of a tile stove for the cabin in Henndorf. It was a gesture entirely in character for a man older than Zuckmayer and already a far more internationally known name after the publication of his extraordinarily evocative account of pre-1914 Europe, *Die Welt von Gestern (The World of Yesterday)*. Like Zuckmayer, his life and career were suddenly capsized by the advent of Nazism. In 1934 Zweig packed a bag and left Vienna for London, never to return. Overcome by a deep depression, he crossed to the New World but found no peace there. In early 1942, while in Brazil, he committed suicide.[12] Then in Vermont, Zuckmayer suffered an agonizing personal loss, which he attempted with some difficulty to express to a friend in English: "I feel as if I would have lost everything again—Henndorf and Salzburg and all the thousand things that were ours in common and tied us up for all times, our language, the faith in our work, the community of spirit and mind—now scattered and exploded and destroyed."[13] The raw quality of that statement makes it clear that no commentary could possibly convey so poignantly Zuckmayer's sorrow and sense of futility.

Less emotional, but not markedly less meaningful, were Zuckmayer's enduring ties with Erich Maria Remarque. At the time that Remarque's sensational bestseller *Im Westen nichts Neues* appeared in 1928, Zuckmayer was completely unacquainted with the author: "I knew nothing of him." They met for the first time in the next year, and he promptly invited Remarque out for "a long wine-soaked night." The two, almost exactly the same age, hit it off at once, and it was the founding of a lifelong friendship. When Remarque's novel became the object of heated controversy, Zuckmayer was quick to defend him: the book, he wrote in the *Berliner Illustrierte Zeitung,* replicated "the truth, pure authentic truth." And he maintained that stance in face of Remarque's critics on the German right who accused him of deprecating the nation's military effort in the First World War. Remarque, he contended, had only recorded the reality known to every young man thrown into hand-to-hand combat: "This is the war as we experienced it on the front." Thus it seemed altogether fitting for Zuckmayer, aging and ailing in 1975, to write: "I was Remarque's oldest—and I believe—best friend since 1929."[14] The extent to which that sentiment was reciprocated should be left to Remarque's biographers.

A survey of Carl Zuckmayer's more intimate personal relationships cannot neglect to inquire about his female lovers, who represented more than a curiosity item in his life and career. The usual story, until now provisionally adopted here, is that after some youthful flirtations in France during the First World War, Zuckmayer had far more intense love affairs with two Annemaries. The first—with Annemarie Ganz—resulted in an unfortunate marriage that quickly ended in divorce; and the second—with Annemarie Seidel—was abruptly cut short by her illness and need for treatment in a Swiss sanatorium. Zuckmayer thereupon met another young actress in Berlin and within three weeks married the woman, Alice Herdan-Zuckmayer, who remained his faithful mate as they lived happily ever after. Such was the implicit message of an encouraging 1925 letter about his bride that Zuckmayer sent to his new mother-in-law: "another wife would not be suitable for me, for my career, and for my entire existence."[15]

Yet Zuckmayer's correspondence tells a somewhat different and more elaborate tale. That he was sexually capable and sometimes quite active as an adult is beyond question. He had proved it, we can recall, during his inglorious theater debut in Kiel after the split from Annemarie Seidel when he sought, as Albrecht Joseph put it, "to dispel his amatory grief with numerous dalliances."[16] Once married, however, throughout the years of exile in Austria and America, Zuckmayer apparently observed the strictest marital fidelity. Two question marks must stand behind that conclusion. One was Annemarie Seidel herself, with whom Zuckmayer maintained a doting and highly affectionate friendship until her death in 1959. In their frequent and often searching letters over the years, they commonly addressed one another as "dearest" and "beloved."[17] In all likelihood, nevertheless, the editor of a volume of their collected correspondence is justified in his assertion: "Although a deep mutual affection is expressed in this correspondence, there is not a question of love letters."[18] Here one must also tread carefully in the case of Käthe Dorsch, especially in the absence of conclusive evidence. Zuckmayer made no secret of his admiration and intense feelings for this beauteous actress whose friendship, as he wrote, "belonged to the major events of my life." Starring in several of Zuckmayer's dramas, she immediately became his ideal stage personality "through the indescribably warm, tender, sublime, and transcendent artistry" of her performances.[19] Accordingly, when writing in 1961 to a perspective biographer, Zuckmayer made clear how much Käthe Dorsch meant to him. He stressed the necessity of crediting her with portrayal of the lead female character in his play *Schinderhannes:* "It was one of her most splendid accomplishments and one of the greatest satisfactions of my theater career. *Absolutely I insist that a picture of her as Julchen be included.*"[20] Such longstanding devotion had for decades stoked rumors that the two were formerly discreet lovers and that they might still be enjoying an occasional secret rendezvous. But those suspicions must remain in the realm of conjecture that will probably never be settled with assurance.

The same is surely not true for two other women with whom Zuckmayer unquestionably had an extended sexual relationship during his marriage. One of them was a third Annemarie! With her Zuckmayer began coupling shortly after the Second World War at a time when he was engaged in a cultural mission for the American government and Alice remained at their Vermont farm. Apart from a few letters exchanged in 1949, nothing is known of Annemarie Hermann. However, Zuckmayer's intimate contacts with her are evidence enough of their complicity, as when he deployed German expressions that scarcely bear translation: *"Liebste," "Entzückende Schöne und Bezaubernde,"* and *"Sehr Liebe und ganz Entzückende"* (roughly: dearest, enchantingly beautiful and bewitching, very dear and totally delightful).[21] Obviously, these are not greetings addressed to a casual acquaintance. They suddenly came to a halt in October 1949 when Zuckmayer attempted to explain his reasons for ending their relationship. It had now become more difficult to maintain once he had met this Annemarie's husband: "What was in the beginning so easy and relaxed between us has now become a burden—especially for you!" It was consequently a load too heavy for them any longer to bear. Almost comically, Zuckmayer concluded this awkward excuse with *"Auf Wiedersehen,"* a farewell that could certainly not be taken literally by his jilted lover.[22]

About the second woman in question even less is known except her name, Ursula Zell, her city of residence, Munich, and her profession, actress. Yet the nature of her close extended relationship with Zuckmayer is no less certain. Their affair began in 1957 and lasted for much of the decade following, as a letter addressed to her by Zuckmayer makes perfectly clear. At the end of 1966 he made a promise to think of her everyday in the next June in order to retain "so much happiness that cannot vanish." It had all started a decade ago "at a more difficult time for you than for me," he stated, and he then added: "I licked the honey and the bitterness—namely the not-having-you-anymore." He recalled Paris ("Rue des Saintes-Pères" [*sic*]), a week in Munich, also Avignon and Marseille. "We had a splendor then that two humans cannot often bestow on one another." The secret of their repeated infidelities, which he had mentioned only to Annemarie Seidel, was in safe keeping. And there is no evidence that Alice ever learned of her husband's extramarital excursions in Europe or that she was troubled by suspicions of them.[23]

The most problematic of Zuckmayer's friends was Bertolt Brecht. In fact, the question eventually arose whether he should consider Brecht a friend at all. The harmonious beginning of their acquaintance did not last, even though they had much in common. Both realized early professional success in the decade after the First World War when Zuckmayer's *Der fröhliche Weinberg* (1925) and Brecht's *Dreigroschenoper* (1929) premiered at the same Schiffbauerdamm Theater in Berlin. Both emigrated to the United

States a decade later: Zuckmayer in 1939, Brecht in 1941. In the early summer of 1945, just as the Second World War was ending, Brecht visited Zuckmayer at his Vermont farm. While Brecht was living in Zürich from 1947 to 1949 Zuckmayer encountered him from time to time at literary gatherings there. During the postwar years both of them reflected and wrote about their overwhelming experience with Nazism: Zuckmayer in *Des Teufels General,* Brecht in *Furcht und Elend des Dritten Reichs* and *Arturo Ui.* As Zuckmayer said: "We rather complemented than excluded one another."[24]

Yet there were two fundamental and, as it proved, unbridgeable differences. One was style. Whereas, following his triumph with *Des Teufels General,* Zuckmayer never recaptured the public imagination as a playwright after 1945, Brecht's star continued to rise, even after his relatively early death in 1956. In the 1960s Zuckmayer thus virtually disappeared from the German stage, while Brecht was hailed and widely performed on both sides of the Atlantic.[25] The other difference was political or, better said, ideological. In the first years of the Weimar Republic, if anything, Zuckmayer was the more engaged of the two, identified as he was with republicanism and socialism. Yet Brecht began to drift more ostentatiously leftward and soon outflanked Zuckmayer by openly espousing Marxism and communism. Much later Zuckmayer summed up perfectly: "In a little obituary for Brecht, with whom I was befriended, I wrote at the time that nothing separated us except theory—which seemed important to him and is unimportant to me."[26]

Assuredly, it is permissible here to suggest a third basic difference. Both in his autobiography and throughout his extensive correspondence over three decades, Zuckmayer made frequent references to Brecht and often found for him words of praise. "In my opinion," Zuckmayer wrote to an editor of the weekly *Die Zeit*, "Brecht was the only true *genius* of our generation."[27] But as one of Zuckmayer's most astute biographers has correctly noted: "to the contrary, the published remarks by Brecht about Zuckmayer are quite meager."[28] Published, one must assume, and also private. After their return to Europe from exile the two maintained a polite distance: "we rather seldom saw one another," Zuckmayer wrote without reproaching Brecht for ignoring him.[29] Then in 1975, nearly twenty years after Brecht's death and shortly before his own, Zuckmayer was asked what he envied about the man who seemed in many ways to be his opposite. "Nothing," Zuckmayer replied. "I only admired him."[30]

It should be evident that these glimpses into Carl Zuckmayer's private life through his letters afford an immediacy not to be found elsewhere. Whatever his circumstances, he always devoted a great deal of time and effort to writing these personal messages. And in later life, aware that he would leave his literary remains to future biographers, he was careful to tuck copies neatly into folders that would be easily accessible to them. Gathered into large bulging archival cartons, these compositions now constitute an indispensable element of the Zuckmayer legacy. Hence they serve to reinforce his more formal writings by revealing details of the inner life of a creative author and observant witness during the most turbulent events of the twentieth century.

POSTSCRIPT

An Odd Couple

It may seem anomalous to add some remarks comparing Carl Zuckmayer with Emst Jünger.[1] Both their professional careers and political views diverged almost as completely as one could imagine, and their experience during the Weimar and Nazi years had little in common. Bedfellows they were not. But during the Second World War, in his secret report to the U.S. War Department, Zuckmayer commented on Jünger, and he did so in the most complimentary of terms: "I consider him to be by far the most talented and important of the authors who have remained in Germany."[2] After 1945 the two men corresponded irregularly, but a meeting between them never took place.[3] Yet it is nonetheless very instructive to examine comparatively this extraordinary pair of personalities who proved to be among the most notable German literary figures of the early twentieth century.[4]

In vain one searches the extant records for a satisfactory explanation of why Zuckmayer and Jünger turned out to be such opposites in so many regards even though their separate family backgrounds were nearly identical. They belonged to exactly the same generation—Jünger was born in March 1895, Zuckmayer just before the end of 1896—which placed their boyhood in the luminous twilight years of the Wilhelmine Reich. For Germany it was a time of rising prosperity and great expectations as the now united nation was rapidly gaining industrial and intellectual preeminence among the states of Europe. Zuckmayer, as mentioned, was securely ensconced in a reasonably affluent bourgeois household, and the same was true of Jünger. Each was located in a middling commercial center in western Germany—Zuckmayer in Mainz, Jünger in Hanover—rather than one of the larger urban cultural conglomerates like Berlin, Hamburg, Frankfurt, or Munich. It was normal for the scions of such families to attend finer primary and secondary schools where they were exposed to a classical curriculum consisting largely of great works by ancient and modern authors. One must observe that neither Zuckmayer nor Jünger was an outstanding pupil and that their rather erratic early education lacked the self-discipline displayed by some of their more assiduous and less rebellious classmates. The fairly predictable result was that the two developed no identifiable intellectual focus as adults. Both became voracious readers, but in a manner that can only be described as random. That much they also had in common.

What is missing in this picture is any deep psychological probing, about which the available sources offer only indistinct hints.

To uncover this crucial factor the historian would presumably need dozens of tape recordings from countless family gatherings, firm bedside instructions from the father, and whispered suggestions from the mother. What was said and what notions were actually conveyed as the child approached manhood? We do not know and shall never learn. Stray autobiographical statements do not yield a solid basis for judgment. Jünger, for example, once remarked that his father was a loving but not particularly affectionate patriarchal figure, and that his mother remained a more remote presence at home—hardly enough to provide a definitive Freudian analysis. In Zuckmayer's case, it could not be inconsequential after 1933 that the forebears on his mother's side were Jewish. Yet he himself devoted little attention to that fact before then, and there is no evidence that it was formative in building his character. Unable to penetrate the recesses of a complex personality, then, we are obliged to rely on external attributes. While Zuckmayer grew to be gregarious to a fault, Jünger was always self-contained and correct, properly dressed whether in uniform or mufti, and emotionally reserved in his dealings with others. Whereas Zuckmayer often stayed up into the wee hours of the morning, carousing with friends, it is difficult to imagine that Jünger frequently indulged himself in such behavior or easily tolerated others who did so. Jünger's self-professed social demeanor was one of *"désinvolture,"* which implied a facade of elitist insouciance on his part that usually precluded intense interaction with his fellows. Thus Zuckmayer's comportment was habitually expansive and extroverted, but Jünger's introverted tendencies habitually kept the common folk and indeed many of his peers at a distance.[5]

All of the foregoing fits neatly into the framework of the pre-1914 German Reich. The impact of the First World War was, even if judged solely in terms of the two authors in question, devastating. Again, their separate experiences as soldiers were remarkably parallel. Both were drafted into military service before graduating from their *Gymnasium* and were consequently awarded a hastily arranged emergency diploma. After some rudimentary training, they were hastened toward the front lines in France where they served throughout the ensuing four years. Both were severely wounded near the war's end. Finally, both received the highest decoration of the German army, *Pour le mérite* (Zuckmayer not until much later). After each was promoted to the rank of lieutenant, they returned to civilian life with physical and psychological scars. They had shared the initial public enthusiasm for the war, suddenly freed as they were from the constraints of bourgeois society, then warming to the camaraderie of bivouacs and battles. So much greater was therefore the disillusionment of defeat. Thus both returned to their mutual homeland disoriented, having no notion whatever of how their life would continue or what their professional career might be.

Still in uniform, neither Zuckmayer nor Jünger participated in the revolution of 1918 that preceded and inaugurated the Weimar Republic. Like many other young veterans, they seemed at first to be displaced persons. Neither made much of an effort to profit from the opportunities for university study, choosing instead to pursue an independent course as a writer and literary figure. They did so during the republican years with considerable success, Jünger as a novelist, Zuckmayer as a playwright. Jünger's *In Stahlgewittern (Storm of Steel)* was published in 1922; Zuckmayer's *Der fröhliche Weinberg* appeared in 1925 and *Der Hauptmann von Köpenick* in 1931.

Yet, despite all of these similarities, the two conspicuously parted company when it came to politics. Accordingly, their positions after 1933 could not have been more at odds. In 1939 Jünger rejoined the German army and, promoted to captain, enjoyed four years as an officer in occupied Paris; whereas Zuckmayer, despised and hounded by the Nazi regime, was forced to endure a long Austrian and American exile. During the Second World War Jünger basked in the prestige earned by his best-selling 1939 novel, *Auf den Marmorklippen (On the Marble Cliffs)*. Meanwhile Zuckmayer withdrew into a silence not broken until the premier and first nationwide performances of *Des Teufels General* in 1946. After the war both had many years to reflect on their long lives and careers. Zuckmayer died in 1977; Jünger, in 1998.

Exploring the daily lives of these two authors reveals another host of similarities and differences. Jünger's major contact with a foreign culture was in France. It began early with a French school exchange program, a curious and largely inconsequential episode in the Foreign Legion, then later his adventures in the two great wars of the early twentieth century. Besides a few affairs with young French women, he had a mistress in Paris for several years, the wife of an incarcerated French journalist. Although Sophie Ravoux was German by birth, she provided Jünger with many contacts in the French capital. While on duty there during the Second World War he also cultivated a wide variety of notable French intellectuals such as Jean Cocteau, Sacha Guitry, Pierre Drieu la Rochelle, Jean Giraudoux, etc. By contrast, he had no direct relationship with Americans before 1945 (excepting an expatriate society hostess named Florence Gould, born of French parents in San Francisco and a veteran resident of Paris), and more than once he referred scornfully to spreading *"Amerikanismus,"* a dismissive term implying mediocrity and vulgarity. By contrast, Carl Zuckmayer's only real contact with the French, apart from their occupation of the Rhineland after 1918, was the result of his wartime experience and his affection for bars and bistros, which also resulted in a series of youthful flirtations. Rather, he well knew Americans. His years of exile in the United States of course gave him a far different perspective on them than that of Jünger, and he was consistently positive in his remarks about them, especially his fellow farmers in

Vermont. By contrast, his brief acquaintance with exiled European intellectuals in New York and Hollywood, like him refugees from the theater world and the film industry of Central Europe, remained with notable exceptions mostly superficial.

A review of the correspondence between Zuckmayer and Jünger provides several clues about their relationship. Although no trace remains of the prewar years, their contacts began well before 1945. In 1938 Zuckmayer explained to Annemarie Seidel that for years he had read Jünger's writings, "which—despite all our differences—repeatedly delight me in style, substance, and thought." He did not care for Jünger's first major novel, *In Stahlgewittern,* yet he recognized that its author was distinguished by traits of "quality, personality, eloquence" matched by very few of their generation.[6] Zuckmayer knew full well of Jünger's deserved reputation as a severe critic of the Weimar Republic, but it would be inadmissible in his view to condemn any German for initially supporting National Socialism or, through a commonplace patriotism, participating in the Second World War. Only the "truly guilty or criminal elements" should be punished.[7] Hence in the late 1950s Zuckmayer made plans with a mutual friend Hans Speidel for the three to meet, which had to be cancelled because of a business trip by Zuckmayer to the United States. He continued nonetheless to hope for a gathering arranged by Speidel. Despite his uncertainty whether Jünger was equally interested in conferring with him, Zuckmayer "could imagine that we have some things to say to each other."[8]

Zuckmayer's positive intentions were confirmed by his relentless campaign, beginning in 1958, to have the ultra-prestigious Goethe Prize awarded to Jünger by the city of Frankfurt. "No matter how one stands on his development over the years," Zuckmayer wrote in oblique reference to Jünger's rightist past, he undoubtedly represented "a great intellectual and linguistic heritage."[9] Zuckmayer pursued that objective for over a decade, complaining to Speidel in 1966 that it was "a shame that Jünger has so far been passed over."[10] By 1970, however, he had to concede that all his efforts had ended in a *"débacle"* because of attacks on Jünger's political past. Even so, Zuckmayer persisted in the conviction that Jünger was "the most important stylist of his generation," a writer of incomparable "literary and intellectual standing."[11]

The question arises again whether Zuckmayer's manifest appreciation of Jünger was reciprocated in kind. We know, for example, that in January 1960 Jünger attended a lecture given by Zuckmayer in Marbach at the celebration of Friedrich Schiller's 200th birthday. He did not come forward after the speech to introduce himself to the speaker, however, but rather sent him a short and enigmatic note that complimented Zuckmayer for offering a message of harmony "in the midst of the dissonances so plentiful in our time."[12] Thus nothing ensued in the 1960s except a few polite exchanges of birthday greetings.[13] The one serious possibility of a meeting occurred in November 1967 on the occasion of Hans Speidel's seventieth birthday in Bad Honnef, near Bonn. It, too, fell through when Zuckmayer suffered an attack of bronchitis. He apologized to Jünger in a note expressing his wish that they finally might foregather in the coming year. "Not yet to have met you," Zuckmayer added, "I consider one of the greatest lacks of my life." Unwilling to be outdone this time, Jünger promptly sent regrets that Zuckmayer's health was *"en panne"* and invited him to visit himself and his wife Liselotte at their family home in the village of Wilflingen during the following January.[14]

Once more the rest was silence, broken only by a cordial invitation to Jünger to visit the Zuckmayers in Saas-Fee: "Now I wish nothing more than that a meeting with you will at last take place." To this, Zuckmayer appended a remark that perfectly epitomized their long and totally botched personal relationship: "It is remarkable that two authors who not only belong to the same generation but also share several interests should first meet on the brink of old age." Even that event failed to materialize. Instead, the final scrap of paper that needs to be recorded here was a brief note in early February 1977 from Jünger to Alice Zuckmayer expressing his condolences at the sad news of her husband's death.[15]

CONCLUSION

Any attempt to reach a summary judgment on the life and career of Carl Zuckmayer should be careful to claim for him neither too much nor too little. Excessive praise would be distorting as well as unconvincing. After all, we are not dealing here with Shakespeare, Goethe, or Molière. A bloated reputation does no service to Zuckmayer's genuine but limited talent. That talent, however, surely deserves recognition and appreciation. It was not accidental that Zuckmayer became one of the most popular—perhaps indeed *the* most popular—European playwright of the early twentieth century. Germans, Austrians, the Swiss, and others voted with their feet as they flocked to theaters throughout Central Europe to enjoy the comic antics of *The Captain of Köpenick* or to bemoan the lamentable fate of *The Devil's General.* For good reason did Zuckmayer become an eminent international presence in the world of theater and cinema.

The incalculable element in the progress of Zuckmayer's professional life was of course the total disruption of it by Nazism. What if the Weimar Republic had survived and he had been able unhindered to continue writing the type of plays like *Der fröhliche Weinberg,* for which he had a remarkable facility? We shall never know. Instead, he was forced into a long brooding isolation far from the excited theater crowds, celebrity gatherings, and stimulating personal contacts with other writers to which he had been accustomed. And once he returned to the rubble, exhaustion, and raw nerves of postwar Europe, he seemed rather out of tune with his surroundings and with the new theater scene that was just beginning to emerge. He was no longer the same man who had departed on a ship from Rotterdam nearly a decade before, and he no longer quite belonged. Quiet and charming as it was, that little farm in Vermont had scarcely prepared him for the distress and dislocation he found around him after 1945.

One reason that has been advanced by his critics for Zuckmayer's inability to sustain his exalted status as a major playwright in the late twentieth century was his failure to develop any overarching philosophy or to take a prominent role in forming and influencing political opinion. There is some obvious truth in this accusation, but it should not go without challenge. To be sure, compared with Germany's best, he was neither an original philosopher like Kant, a political theorist like Hegel, nor a macroeconomist like Karl Marx. Yet he did embody an identifiable standpoint as a quiet and steady republican. Hence his sometimes outspoken rejection of ideological extremes, his public support for the Weimar Republic, and his unfailing patriotism. The collapse of those values in 1933 suddenly left Zuckmayer, like millions of others, adrift and rudderless in turbulent waters. There was little opportunity for him to regain a firmer emotional footing while being pursued by the Gestapo. And there was no possibility for him to make a meaningful contribution to the German resistance movement from a rural village in Vermont. Zuckmayer's overriding response to postwar Germany was thus one of confusion as he moved about in a devastated homeland that was hardly recognizable to him. The anguished words of Wilhelm Voigt come quickly to mind: "Where is the *Heimat...?* I no longer see a *Heimat!"*

It is probably in this perspective that one can best evaluate the contribution of Carl Zuckmayer. He should be placed with such authors as Thomas Mann, Erich Maria Remarque, and Bertolt Brecht, whose life and work were immensely clouded by the sprawling shadow of Adolf Hitler. German intellectuals of their generation and anti-fascist persuasion had no realistic alternative to exile, generally in the United States, and they could never again be fully reconciled to their former homeland. Finally they came to live in an emotional estrangement from which there was no return. Altogether fitting for Carl Zuckmayer in the end was thus a marvelous Alpine refuge in Switzerland.

NOTES

Preface

[1] Carl Zuckmayer, *Als wär's ein Stück von mir* (Frankfurt-am-Main and Vienna, 1966), p. 439. Unless otherwise indicated, all details and quotations in Part One of this biography are taken from these memoirs. An English translation appeared later: *A Part of Myself. Portrait of an Epoch* (New York, 1970). But no reader of German could possibly overlook a surely intended pun, since *Stück* can also refer to a stage play. Hence an equally plausible translation of the title might be: *As if it were one of my plays.*

[2] Allan Mitchell, *The Devil's Captain. Ernst Jünger in Nazi Paris, 1941–1944* (New York and Oxford, 2011).

Chapter One

[1] Zuckmayer, *Als wär's ein Stück von mir*, p. 137.

[2] Ibid., p. 173.

[3] Ibid., p. 182.

[4] Ibid., p. 222.

[5] Ibid., p. 230.

[6] Ibid., p. 247.

[7] Ibid., p. 250.

[8] Ibid., p. 251.

[9] Ibid., pp. 255-56.

Chapter Two

1   Zuckmayer, *Als wär's ein Stück von mir*, p. 307.

2   Ibid., p. 310.

3   Ibid., p. 314.

4   Ibid., p. 348. In a letter he wrote: "I am alone, for the first time again totally alone, and feel myself in regard to fate, future, and women like sixteen." Zuckmayer to Annemarie Seidel, September 25, 1922, DLA Marbach.

5   Zuckmayer, *Als wär's ein Stück von mir*, pp. 384–85.

6   Zuckmayer, *Kreuzweg. Drama* (Munich, 1921). Zuckmayer to Annemarie Seidel, August 20, 1924, DLA Marbach.

7   Zuckmayer, *Als wär's ein Stück von mir*, p. 311.

8   Ibid., p. 323.

9   Ibid., p. 324.

10   Ibid., pp. 348–54.

11   Ibid., pp. 368–72. Zuckmayer, "Der Eunuch," in *Jahrbuch zur Literatur der Weimarer Republik,* vol. 3 (1997), pp. 47–122.

12   Zuckmayer, *Als wär's ein Stück von mir*, p. 382.

13   Ibid., pp. 394–96. Zuckmayer, *Pankraz erwacht oder Die Hinterwäldler* (Berlin, 1925).

14   Zuckmayer, *Der fröhliche Weinberg. Lustspiel in drei Akten* (Berlin, 1925).

15   Zuckmayer, *Als wär's ein Stück von mir*, pp. 412–13.

16   Ibid., pp. 367, 423–24. Zuckmayer, *Der fröhliche Weinberg. Schinderhannes. Zwei Stücke* (2nd ed.; Frankfurt-am-Main, 2004). Zuckmayer, *Katharina Knie* (2nd ed.; Frankfurt-am-Main, 2004).

17   Zuckmayer, *Der Hauptmann von Köpenick. Ein deutsches Märchen in drei Akten* (6th ed.; Frankfurt-am-Main, 1980). Zuckmayer, *Als wär's ein Stück von mir*, pp. 439–45. One friend wrote: in Essen "we have recorded

a success such as never before in my lifetime." There the new play was
performed fifty times between March and June 1931. Hans Kupper to
Zuckmayer, March 24 and June 20, 1931, DLA Marbach.

[18] Zuckmayer to Albrecht Joseph, July 18, 1931, ibid.

Chapter Three

[1] Zuckmayer, *Als wär's ein Stück von mir*, p. 47.

[2] Ibid., p. 60. *See* Christian Strasser, *Carl Zuckmayer: Deutscher Künstler im Salzburger Exil 1933–1938* (Vienna, Cologne, Weimar, 1996).

[3] Zuckmayer, *Bellman. Schauspiel in drei Akten* (Chur, 1938).

[4] Zuckmayer, *Als wär's ein Stück von mir*, p. 74.

[5] Ibid., p. 80.

[6] Ibid., p. 95. Zuckmayer to Dorothy Thompson, December 19, 1938, DLA Marbach.

[7] Zuckmayer, *Als wär's ein Stück von mir*, p. 99.

[8] Ibid., p. 103.

[9] Ibid., p. 106.

[10] Ibid., p. 117.

[11] Ibid., p. 120. Zuckmayer to Albrecht Joseph, October 4, 1938, DLA Marbach. Zuckmayer to Hans Schweikert, February 28, 1966, ibid.

[12] Zuckmayer, *Als wär's ein Stück von mir*, p. 120.

[13] Zuckmayer to Gottfried Bermann-Fischer, April 11, 1938, DLA Marbach.

[14] Zuckmayer, *Als wär's ein Stück von mir*, p. 122.

[15] Ibid., p. 124.

[16] Ibid., pp. 465–67.

Chapter Four

[1] Zuckmayer, *Als wär's ein Stück von mir*, pp. 486–87.

[2] Ibid. Zuckmayer to Annemarie Seidel, June 8, 1939, DLA Marbach.

[3] Zuckmayer, *Als wär's ein Stück von mir*, p. 487. Zuckmayer to Albrecht Joseph, July 21, 1940, DLA Marbach.

[4] Zuckmayer, *Als wär's ein Stück von mir*, p. 498.

[5] Ibid., p. 502. Meanwhile, Zuckmayer signed a contract with Harcourt and Brace Publishers to write two novels and a work of non-fiction (never completed). Zuckmayer to Paul Schoenfeld, December 13, 1941, DLA Marbach.

[6] Zuckmayer, *Als wär's ein Stück von mir*, pp. 517–18.

[7] Alice Herdan-Zuckmayer, *Die Farm in den grünen Bergen* (4th ed.; Frankfurt-am-Main, 2008), p. 27.

[8] Ibid., p. 91. Zuckmayer to Albrecht Joseph, January 15 and July 25, 1942, DLA Marbach.

[9] Herdan-Zuckmayer, *Die Farm in den grünen Bergen*, p. 224. Zuckmayer, *Des Teufels General. Drama in drei Akten* (Stockholm, 1946).

[10] Zuckmayer, *Als wär's ein Stück von mir*, pp. 525–26.

[11] Ibid., p. 530. Zuckmayer to Max Bondy, October 20, 1943, DLA Marbach.

[12] Zuckmayer to Rudolf and Helene Aeschlimann, November 30, 1942, ibid.

[13] Zuckmayer, *Als wär's ein Stück von mir*, pp. 536–37.

[14] See "Die Entstehung von Zuckmayers 'Geheimreport'" in Zuckmayer, *Geheimreport* (3rd ed.; Göttingen, 2002), pp. 453–55. This volume has been expertly edited by Gunther Nickel and Johanna Schrön.

[15] Ibid., pp. 10–12.

[16] Ibid., p. 46.

[17] Ibid., p. 57.

[18]   Ibid., p. 76.

[19]   Ibid., pp. 93–94.

[20]   Ibid., pp. 127–28.

[21]   Zuckmayer, *Als wär's ein Stück von mir,* p. 538.

Chapter Five

[1]   Carl Zuckmayer, *Deutschlandbericht für das Kriegsministerium der Vereinigten Staaten von Amerika* (2nd ed.; Frankfurt-am-Main, 2007), edited by Gunther Nickel, Johanna Schrön, and Hans Wagener.

[2]   Ibid., p. 69.

[3]   Ibid., p. 141. Zuckmayer, *Als wär's ein Stück von mir,* pp. 546–48.

[4]   Ibid., pp. 548–50.

[5]   Ibid., pp. 553–54. Zuckmayer, *Deutschlandbericht,* pp. 107–14.

[6]   Ibid., p. 229.

[7]   Ibid., pp. 237–38.

[8]   Ibid., p. 212.

[9]   Ibid., p. 79.

[10]   Ibid., p. 90.

[11]   Ibid., pp. 90–91.

[12]   Ibid., pp. 156–57.

[13]   Ibid., p. 197.

[14]   Ibid., pp. 102–103.

[15]   Zuckmayer, *Als wär's ein Stück von mir,* p. 559.

[16]   Zuckmayer to Henry Goverts, October 25, 1945, MLA Marbach.

[17]   Zuckmayer to Pare and Elizabeth Lorentz, August 12, 1948, ibid.

[18]   Zuckmayer to George Marton, January 18, 1958, ibid.

[19]   Zuckmayer to John MacDill, January 26 and October 20, 1958, ibid.

20 Zuckmayer to the American consulate in Salzburg, August 4, 1958, ibid.

21 Zuckmayer to Hermann Kesten, November 1, 1962, ibid.

22 Zuckmayer, *Als wär's ein Stück von mir,* pp. 567–73.

23 *See* Werner Imsang, *Carl Zuckmayer in Saas-Fee. Ein Album* (3ʳᵈ ed.; Zürich, 1982).

Chapter Six

1 Zuckmayer's most diligent biographer has counted his literary production from 1920 to 1955, in addition to his thirteen plays, at more than ninety poems, ten novellas *(Erzählungen),* three novels, five long essays, nine film scripts, and over a hundred published articles in newspapers and magazines. Arnold John Jacobius, *Motive und Dramaturgie im Schauspiel Carl Zuckmayers* (Frankfurt-am-Main, 1971), p. 6.

2 Zuckmayer, *Kreuzweg,* p. 5.

3 Zuckmayer to Egon Raushofen-Wertheimer, May 26, 1920, DLA Marbach.

4 Zuckmayer to Ingeborg Engelsing-Malek, [?] August 1960, ibid.; Zuckmayer to J.P. Brejoux, March 14, 1962, ibid.

5 Zuckmayer to Ingeborg Brandt, October 1, 1976, ibid.

6 Zuckmayer, *Der fröhliche Weinberg,* p. 10.

7 Ibid., p. 11.

8 Ibid., p. 13.

9 Ibid., pp. 43–44.

10 Ibid., pp. 48–50.

11 Ibid., p. 66.

12 Zuckmayer to Edith Hennig, [?] 1958, DLA Marbach; Zuckmayer to Carl Bengard, August 26, 1972, ibid.

13 Zuckmayer, *Schinderhannes,* pp. 88–93.

[14]   Ibid., pp. 57–58.

[15]   Ibid., pp. 123–24.

[16]   Ibid., p. 127.

[17]   Ibid., p. 138.

[18]   Ibid., pp. 158–66.

[19]   Zuckmayer, *Katharina Knie,* pp. 103–104, 115.

[20]   Ibid., p. 147.

[21]   Ibid., p. 159.

[22]   Ibid., p. 178.

[23]   Ibid., pp. 181–83.

[24]   Ibid., p. 185.

[25]   Ibid., pp. 188–89.

[26]   Ibid., p. 193.

[27]   Ibid., p. 197.

Chapter Seven

[1]   Zuckmayer to Marta Maria Gehrke, February 18, 1949, DLA Marbach; Zuckmayer to Rudolf and Ines Müller Horn, March 31, 1965, ibid.; Zuckmayer to Audrey Davis, February 12, 1970, ibid.

[2]   Zuckmayer, *Der Hauptmann von Köpenick,* p. 17.

[3]   Ibid., p. 22.

[4]   Ibid., p. 35.

[5]   Ibid., p. 41.

[6]   Ibid., p. 62.

[7]   Ibid., pp. 88–90.

[8]   Ibid., p. 107.

[9]   Ibid., pp. 116–20.

[10]   Ibid., p. 128.

[11]   Zuckmayer, *Des Teufels General,* p. 9.

[12]   Ibid., p. 13.

[13]   Ibid., p. 17.

[14]   Ibid., p. 25. Zuckmayer later expanded on this thought. He did not see Harras as a "noble type of the correct old soldiers," he wrote, but simply as an airplane pilot. He thought the movie actor Curd Jürgens was perfect for the part (which he played in the most notable film version). Zuckmayer to Hannes Tannert, December 14, 1962, DLA Marbach.

[15]   Zuckmayer, *Des Teufels General,* pp. 39–43.

[16]   Ibid., p. 67.

[17]   Zuckmayer, *Als wär's ein Stück mir,* pp. 534–36.

[18]   He admitted later that the Lawrence character could just as well be omitted in a more abbreviated staging for school children. Zuckmayer to Dr. Langer (Austrian Ministry of Instruction), June 28, 1962, DLA Marbach.

[19]   Zuckmayer, *Des Teufels General,* pp. 92–95.

[20]   Ibid., pp. 96–98.

[21]   Ibid., pp. 120–21.

[22]   Ibid., pp. 127–28.

[23]   Ibid., pp. 143–45.

[24]   Ibid., p. 149.

[25]   Ibid., p. 155.

[26]   In particular, Zuckmayer had to admit that the role of Oderbruch was "problematic," because he was inadequately "filled with life" so as to become "a completely convincing character." Zuckmayer to Hiltrud Arlauf, January 15, 1955, DLA Marbach.

Chapter Eight

1 Zuckmayer to Shepard Stone, January 15, 1950, ibid.

2 Zuckmayer to Anita Daniel, January 12, 1962, ibid.; Zuckmayer to Alice Wegmann, February 17, 1966, ibid.

3 Zuckmayer to Ilse Langner, August 28, 1970, ibid.; Zuckmayer to Willi Kollo, December 28, 1970, ibid.

4 Zuckmayer to Arnold John Jacobius, April 8 and July 22, 1964, ibid.; Zuckmayer to Alice Frohlich, January 17, 1965, ibid.

5 Zuckmayer to Joachim Maass, March 16, 1965, ibid.; Zuckmayer to Hermann Dollinger, January 21, 1966, ibid.

6 Generally, on this topic *see* Ausma Balinkin, *The Central Women Figures in Carl Zuckmayer's Dramas* (diss.; University of Cincinnati, 1976).

Chapter Nine

1 Zuckmayer to Albrecht Joseph, January 4 and 12, 1923, DLA Marbach.

2 Zuckmayer to Albrecht Joseph, [?] 1920, ibid.

3 Zuckmayer to Claire Liesenberg, December 11, 1923, ibid.

4 Zuckmayer to Albrecht Joseph, February 17, 1931, ibid. Zuckmayer to Hannes Kupper, March 16 and 31, 1931, ibid. Zuckmayer to Hans Schiebelhuth, April 27, 1931, ibid.

5 Zuckmayer, "Mein Leben in dreissig Zeilen," *Frankfurter General-Anzeiger,* June 23, 1928.

6 Zuckmayer to Dr. Jacobs, March 24, 1929, DLA Marbach.

7 Zuckmayer to the *Vossische Zeitung,* June 15, 1930, ibid. Zuckmayer to Benjamin Hübsch, June 16, 1932, ibid.

8 Zuckmayer to Sybille Bänder, August 8, 1938, ibid.

9 Zuckmayer to Benjamin Hübsch, July 9, 1940, ibid.

[10] Zuckmayer to Eva Noack, October 18, 1948, ibid.

[11] Zuckmayer to Gunther Fleckenstein, April 29, 1976, ibid.

[12] Zuckmayer to Annemarie [Seidel] Suhrkamp, May 18, 1930, ibid.

[13] Zuckmayer, *Als wär's ein Stück von mir,* pp. 254–55.

[14] Zuckmayer to Ina Seidel, [?] 1922, DLA Marbach.

[15] Zuckmayer to Albrecht Joseph, June 16, 1928, ibid.; Zuckmayer to Hans Schiebelhuth, April 9, 1931, ibid.; Zuckmayer to Albrecht Joseph, May 1, 1931, and April 8, 1932, ibid.; Zuckmayer to Hannes Kupper, May 4, 1931, ibid.

[16] Zuckmayer to Eva Noack, March 23, 1949, ibid.; Zuckmayer to Ludwig Berger, August 13, 1949, September 25, 1965, and January 14, 1969, ibid.

[17] Zuckmayer to Joachim Maass, January 4, 1946, ibid.

[18] Zuckmayer to Peter Suhrkamp, November 16, 1948, ibid.; Zuckmayer to Hanns Niedecken-Gebhardt, November 20, 1948, ibid.; Zuckmayer to Marta Maria Gehrke, February 18, 1949, ibid.; Zuckmayer to Emmy Rado, March 7, 1949, ibid.

[19] Zuckmayer to Antoinette Knie, August 15, 1949, ibid.; Zuckmayer to Jost Weigold, November 25, 1949, ibid.; Zuckmayer to Shepard Stone, June 15, 1950, ibid.

[20] Zuckmayer to Hans Schalla, May 28, 1957, ibid.; Zuckmayer to Sheila Rooke, June 16, 1963, ibid.

[21] Zuckmayer to Rudolf and Helene Aeschlimann, March 31, 1965, ibid.; Zuckmayer to Jan Schlerbad, July 3, 1965, ibid.; Zuckmayer to Carl Raddatz, May 31, 1966, ibid.

[22] Zuckmayer to Herbert Bohlinger, August 25, 1966, ibid.; Zuckmayer to Helen Wolff, June 29, 1967, ibid.; Zuckmayer to Hannes Reinhardt, October 3, 1967, ibid.

23 All of these and more can be gathered from the Deutsches Literaturarchiv in Marbach. To cite a few examples: Zuckmayer to Joseph Clavs, October 29, 1968, ibid.; Zuckmayer to Wolfgang Schaffler, April 1, 1971, ibid.; Zuckmayer to Hans Lechner, September 25, 1975, ibid.; Zuckmayer to Hans-Dietrich Genscher, February 9, 1976, ibid.; Zuckmayer to Günther Fleckenstein, April 29, 1976, ibid.

Chapter Ten

1 See Gunther Nickel (ed.), *Carl Zuckmayer, Albrecht Joseph. Briefwechsel 1922–1972* (Göttingen, 2007).

2 Albrecht Joseph, *Portraits 1. Carl Zuckmayer-Bruno Frank* (Aachen, 1993), p. 240.

3 Ibid., p. 44.

4 Zuckmayer, *Als wär's ein Stück von mir,* p. 438.

5 Quoted by William Grange, *Partnerschaft in the German Theater. Zuckmayer and Hilpert* (New York, 1991), p. 36.

6 Thomas Mann to Zuckmayer, May 24, 1932, DLA Marbach.

7 Zuckmayer to Tankred Dorst, July 29, 1966, ibid.

8 Zuckmayer to Günter Grass, July 1, 1969, ibid.

9 Zuckmayer to Karl Barth, July 10 and October 9, 1967, and April 10, 1968, ibid. *See* Heinrich Stoevesandt (ed.), *Späte Freundschaft. Carl Zuckmayer, Karl Barth in Briefen (5th ed.;* Zürich, 1979).

10 Zuckmayer to Theodor Reuss, July 5, 1956, and July 14, 1960, ibid.

11 Zuckmayer to Oskar Kokoschka, [?] 1967, ibid. Zuckmayer, *Als wär's ein Stück von mir,* pp. 299–300.

12 Ibid., pp. 49–54.

13 Zuckmayer to Benjamin Hübsch, February 26, 1942, DLA Marbach.

[14] Zuckmayer, *Aufruf zum Leben. Porträts und Zeugnisse aus bewegten Zeiten* (Frankfurt-am-Main,1976), pp. 93–97. Zuckmayer to the Bayerischer Rundfunk, January 22, 1975, DLA Marbach.

[15] Zuckmayer to Claire Liesenberg, December 11, 1925, ibid. See Zuckmayer, "Wiedersehen mit einer Stadt. Aus dem Stegreif erzählt im Dezember 1968," *Auf einem Weg im Frühling* (Salzburg, 1970), pp. 23–56.

[16] Joseph, *Portraits,* p. 10.

[17] For instance, Zuckmayer to Annemarie Seidel, August 3, 1938, and September 26, 1940, DLA Marbach.

[18] Gunther Nickel (ed.), *"Persönlich—wär so unendlich viel zu sagen": Der Briefwechsel zwischen Carl Zuckmayer und Annemarie Seidel* (St. Ingbert, 1999), p. 9.

[19] Zuckmayer, *Als wär's ein Stück von mir,* pp. 170, 423.

[20] Zuckmayer to Ludwig Reindl, January 8, 1961, DLA Marbach.

[21] Zuckmayer to Annemarie Hermann, September 11, 14, and 25, 1949, ibid.

[22] Zuckmayer to Annemarie Hermann, October 16, 1949, ibid.

[23] Zuckmayer to Ursula Zell, December 14, 1966, ibid.

[24] Zuckmayer to Rudolf W. Leonhardt, April 4, 1962, ibid.

[25] See Nickel, "Zuckmayer und Brecht," *Jahrbuch der deutschen Schillergesellschaft* 41 (1997): 428–59.

[26] Zuckmayer to Professor Reinbold, January 3, 1961, DLA Marbach.

[27] Zuckmayer to Rudolf W. Leonhardt, March 24, 1965, ibid.

[28] Siegfried Mews, "'Der Brecht zeugte den Zuckmayer': Zum persönlichen und literarischen Verhältnis Brechts und Zuckmayers," in Richard Albrecht (ed.), "Facetten der internationalen Carl-Zuckmayer-Forschung," in *Blätter der Carl-Zuckmayer-Gesellschaft* 18 (1997): 58.

29 Adelbert Reif, "Der Mensch ist das Mass. Ein Gespräch mit Carl Zuckmayer," ibid., p. 11.

30 Quoted by Nickel, "Zuckmayer und Brecht," p. 459.

Postscript

1 On the latter, see Allan Mitchell, *The Devil's Captain. Ernst Jünger in Nazi Paris, 1941–1944* (New York and Oxford, 2011).

2 Zuckmayer, *Geheimreport*, p. 102.

3 Ibid., p. 310.

4 This postscript should be compared with and supplemented by an essay by Gunther Nickel, "Ihnen bisher nicht begegnet zu sein, empfinde ich als einen der grössten Mängel in meinem Leben." Der Briefwechsel Carl Zuckmayer und Ernst Jünger," in Hans Wagener (ed.), *Zuckmayer-Jahrbuch* 2 (1999): 515–47.

5 Mitchell, *The Devil's Captain*, pp. 90–91.

6 Zuckmayer to Annemarie Seidel, November 27, 1938, DLA Marbach.

7 Zuckmayer to Willy Umminger, April 28, 1948, ibid.

8 Zuckmayer to Hans Speidel, April 8 and November 16, 1955, ibid.

9 Zuckmayer to W. Bockelmann (mayor of Frankfurt), March 3, 1958, ibid.

10 Zuckmayer to Hans Speidel, March 10, 1966, ibid.

11 Zuckmayer to Professor Emil Staiger, January 1, 1970, ibid.; Zuckmayer to Willi Brundert (mayor of Frankfurt), April 12, 1970, ibid.

12 Ernst Jünger to Zuckmayer, January 19, 1960, ibid.

13 Zuckmayer to Ernst Jünger, March 29, 1965, ibid.; Ernst Jünger to Zuckmayer, December 26, 1966, ibid.; Zuckmayer to Ernst Jünger, March 21, 1967, ibid.

14   Zuckmayer to Ernst Jünger, November 14, 1967, ibid.; Ernst Jünger to Zuckmayer, November 15, 1967, ibid.

15   Ernst Jünger to Alice Zuckmayer, February 3, 1977, ibid.

SELECTED BIBLIOGRAPHY

Ayck, Thomas. *Carl Zuckmayer in Selbstzeugnissen und Bilddokumenten* (Hamburg, 1977).

Balinkin, Ausma. *The Central Women Figures in Carl Zuckmayer's Dramas* (PhD dissertation, University of Cincinnati, 1976).

Bauer, Arnold. *Carl Zuckmayer* (2nd ed.; Berlin, 1977).

Becker, Jochen. *Carl Zuckmayer und seine Heimaten. Ein Album* (3rd ed.; Mainz, 1984).

Burrick, Raymond Erford. *A Characterization of the Mystical Philosophy of Carl Zuckmayer as Revealed in his Life and Works* (PhD dissertation, Tulane University, 1964).

Engelsing-Malek, Ingeborg. *"Amor Fati" in Zuckmayers Dramen* (Berkeley, Los Angeles, Konstanz, 1960).

Finke, Margot. *Carl Zuckmayer's Germany* (Frankfurt-am-Main, 1990).

Frizen, Werner. *Carl Zuckmayer, Der Hauptmann von Köpenick: Interpretation* (Munich, 1988).

Gehrke, Hans. *Carl Zuckmayer. Der Hauptmann von Köpenick. Interpretation und Materialien* (2nd ed.; Hollfeld, 1994).

Glade, Henry. *The Concept of Humanität in the Life and Works of Carl Zuckmayer* (PhD dissertation, University of Pennsylvania, 1958).

Glauert, Barbara (ed.). *Carl Zuckmayer. Das Bühnenwerk im Spiegel der Kritik* (Frankfurt-am-Main, 1977).

Grange, William. *Partnerschaft in the German Theater. Zuckmayer and Hilpert, 1925–1961* (New York, 1991).

Imsang, Werner. *Carl Zuckmayer in Saas-Fee. Ein Album* (3rd ed.; Zürich, 1982).

Jacobius, Arnold John. *Motive und Dramaturgie im Schauspiel Carl Zuckmayers* (Frankfurt-am Main, 1971).

Kieser, Harro (ed.). *Carl Zuckmayer. Materialien zu Leben und Werk* (Frankfurt-am-Main, 1986).

Lange, Rudolf. *Carl Zuckmayer* (Hanover, 1969).

Meinherz, Paul. *Carl Zuckmayer. Sein Weg zu einem modernen Schauspiel* (Bern, 1960).

Mews, Siegfried. *Carl Zuckmayer* (Boston, 1981).

_____. *Carl Zuckmayer, Des Teufels General* (3rd ed.; Frankfurt-am-Main, 1987).

Strasser, Christian. *Carl Zuckmayer. Deutscher Künstler im Salzburger Exil 1933–1938* (Vienna, Cologne, Weimar, 1996).

Reindl, Ludwig Emanuel. *Zuckmayer. Eine Bibliographie* (Munich, 1962).

Wagener, Hans. *Carl Zuckmayer* (Munich, 1983).

_____. *Carl Zuckmayer, Criticism: Tracing Endangered Fame* (Columbia, S.C., 1995).

Wemhoff,Sebastian. *Der Dramatiker und seine Welttragödie. Carl Zuckmayers Gesellschaftsbild und seine Sicht auf den Nationalsozialismus* (Münster, 2010).

ZUCKMAYER'S PLAYS CITED

Kreuzweg (1920), 21, 78-80, 83, 111

Pankraz erwacht (1925), 25

Der fröhliche Weinberg (1925), 25-28, 31, 80-84, 88, 93, 105, 111, 117-118,

   136, 143, 148

Schinderhannes (1927), 27, 84-88, 93, 133

Katharina Knie (1928), 27, 88-93, 95

Der Hauptmann von Köpenick (1931), 27-28, 31, 50, 62, 93-98, 105, 108, 111,

   117, 119, 128, 143, 148

Bellman (1938), 32, 35, 37, 59

Des Teufels General (1946), 46, 59, 62, 98-105, 107-108, 111-113, 119, 121,

   127, 136, 143, 148

Barbara Blomberg (1949), 119

Der Gesang im Feuerofen (1953), 107-109

Das Leben des Horace A. W. Tabor (1964), 108-109

Kranichtanz (1967), 119

NAME INDEX

SUBJECT INDEX

Also by Allan Mitchell

Books

1) *Revolution in Bavaria, 1918–1919. The Eisner Regime and the Soviet Republic* (1965)

2) German translation: *Revolution in Bayern 1918/19. Die Eisner-Regierung und die Räterepublik* (1967)

3) *Bismarck and the French Nation, 1848–1890* (1971)

4) *The German Influence in France after 1870: The Formation of the French Republic* (1979)

5) *Victors and Vanquished: The German Influence on Army and Church in France after 1870* (1984)

6) *The Divided Path: The German Influence on Social Reform in France after 1870* (1991)

7) *The Great Train Race: Railways and the Franco-German Rivalry, 1815–1914* (2000)

8) *Rêves Parisiens: L 'échec de projets de transport public en France au XIXe siècle* (2005)

9) *A Stranger in Paris: Germany's Role in Republican France, 1870–1940* (2006)

10) *Nazi Paris: The History of an Occupation, 1940–1944* (2008)

191

11) *The Devil's Captain: Ernst Jünger in Nazi Paris, 1941–1944* (2011)

12) *Witnessing Postwar Europe: The Personal History of an American Abroad* (2011)

13) *Fleeing Nazi Germany: Five Historians Migrate to America* (2011)

14) *Socialism and the Emergence of the Welfare State* (2012)

Anthologies

1. *Everyman in Europe: Essays in Social History,* 2 vols. (3rd ed., 1990) with Istvan Deak

2. *Bourgeois Society in Nineteenth-Century Europe* (2nd ed., 1993) with Jürgen Kocka

3. *The Nazi Revolution: Hitler's Dictatorship and the German Nation* (4th ed., 1997)

Printed in the United States
By Bookmasters